解析路德维希·维特根斯坦
《哲学研究》

AN ANALYSIS OF
LUDWIG WITTGENSTEIN'S
PHILOSOPHICAL
INVESTIGATIONS

Michael O' Sullivan ◎ 著

杨晓波 ◎ 译

目　录

引　言 ……………………………………………… 1
　　路德维希·维特根斯坦其人　　　　　　　　　 2
　　《哲学研究》的主要内容　　　　　　　　　　　3
　　《哲学研究》的学术价值　　　　　　　　　　　4

第一部分：学术渊源 ……………………………… 7
　　1. 作者生平与历史背景　　　　　　　　　　　 8
　　2. 学术背景　　　　　　　　　　　　　　　　12
　　3. 主导命题　　　　　　　　　　　　　　　　16
　　4. 作者贡献　　　　　　　　　　　　　　　　21

第二部分：学术思想 ……………………………… 25
　　5. 思想主脉　　　　　　　　　　　　　　　　26
　　6. 思想支脉　　　　　　　　　　　　　　　　31
　　7. 历史成就　　　　　　　　　　　　　　　　36
　　8. 著作地位　　　　　　　　　　　　　　　　41

第三部分：学术影响 ……………………………… 47
　　9. 最初反响　　　　　　　　　　　　　　　　48
　　10. 后续争议　　　　　　　　　　　　　　　 52
　　11. 当代印迹　　　　　　　　　　　　　　　 56
　　12. 未来展望　　　　　　　　　　　　　　　 59

术语表 ……………………………………………… 63
人名表 ……………………………………………… 66

CONTENTS

WAYS IN TO THE TEXT	73
Who Was Ludwig Wittgenstein?	74
What Does *Philosophical Investigations* Say?	75
Why Does *Philosophical Investigations* Matter?	77
SECTION 1: INFLUENCES	81
Module 1: The Author and the Historical Context	82
Module 2: Academic Context	87
Module 3: The Problem	92
Module 4: The Author's Contribution	98
SECTION 2: IDEAS	103
Module 5: Main Ideas	104
Module 6: Secondary Ideas	110
Module 7: Achievement	116
Module 8: Place in the Author's Work	121
SECTION 3: IMPACT	127
Module 9: The First Responses	128
Module 10: The Evolving Debate	133
Module 11: Impact and Influence Today	138
Module 12: Where Next?	142
Glossary of Terms	147
People Mentioned in the Text	150
Works Cited	155

引 言

要 点

- 路德维希·维特根斯坦（1889—1951）是奥地利哲学家，也是 20 世纪最重要的思想家之一。
- 《哲学研究》出版于 1953 年，讨论了语言、人类的心智，以及哲学的本质。
- 《哲学研究》是维特根斯坦后期哲学的集大成之作，也是语言哲学与心灵哲学领域迄今最为重要、影响最大的著作之一。

路德维希·维特根斯坦其人

路德维希·维特根斯坦 1889 年出生于奥地利维也纳。他年轻时学习的是工程学，但这一领域的数学工作培养了他对数学哲学的兴趣，进而他又将兴趣推广到了一般哲学。维特根斯坦阅读了哲学家伯特兰·罗素*的《数学原则》，对其十分崇拜。1911 年，他前往英格兰，在剑桥大学问学于罗素门下，但在第一次世界大战*期间离开了剑桥，奔赴前线为奥地利而战。战争期间他完成了一部哲学著作，即《逻辑哲学论》[1]，这本书产生了巨大的影响。该书致力于揭示语言与世界是如何关联的，并解释我们的词句是如何获得意义的。维特根斯坦相信，此时他已解决了哲学的主要问题，于是放弃了哲学，在奥地利当了一名小学教员。

1929 年，维特根斯坦重返剑桥任教，从此开启了他哲学思考的新阶段。在那里，他对之前深信不疑的许多东西提出了质疑，包括《逻辑哲学论》里的一些观点。此时，他认为《逻辑哲学论》对语言的解释已严重偏离了我们使用语言的日常经验。

然而，维特根斯坦未将他的新思想在其有生之年出版，只是拿来与朋友和学生们一起讨论。他想写一部书来表述这些思想，为此写下了很多本笔记与草稿，不过他对自己所写的并不十分满意。他的学生们将包含在《哲学研究》题下的材料汇编成册并进行了编辑，在他1951年逝世之后，该书得以出版。

与《逻辑哲学论》一样，《哲学研究》也在哲学中催生了一个新的思想流派。如今，维特根斯坦已被公认为20世纪最伟大的思想家之一，许多人将《哲学研究》视为他最优秀的作品。

《哲学研究》的主要内容

维特根斯坦的《哲学研究》出版于1953年，这是一本相当复杂的著作。在书中，维特根斯坦并未聚焦于一个论题，而是涉猎了多个主题，其中最重要的主题是语言。他相信哲学问题源于语言使用的混乱，解决之道乃澄清语言的使用——而非发现新的事实或创造新的理论。

《哲学研究》提供了一种不同于传统的思考哲学的方式。哲学家们常常自以为在构建关于世界的普遍理论，维特根斯坦认为这是个错误。他也质疑了在他写作《哲学研究》时所流行的一种信念，即相信科学能解决一切重要的心智问题。在他看来，哲学问题与科学问题有很大的不同，前者不能通过对世界有更多发现来解决。

维特根斯坦认为，如果我们想理解语言和心灵，那就必须考察语言的日常用法。我们必须考察人们是如何在日常生活中使用语言的，这在不同的社会与文化中有很大差别。因此，当维特根斯坦问道："一个词或一句话的意义是什么？"他的回答是："词句的意义在于它在语言中的用法。"换言之，为了理解意义，我们必须考察不同的人、不同的文化与社群是如何使用词句的，因为意义在本质上是公共的、社会的现象。

维特根斯坦批评了德国数学家、哲学家戈特洛布·弗雷格*等人的观点，他们认为意义是抽象的。与之相反，维特根斯坦主张是日常生活的需要决定了我们使用词句的方式。他说，我们用语言来开玩笑、买食物或玩游戏。抽象的规则不能主宰我们使用语言的方式，而且，从前人们使用语言的方式并不能告诉我们当下如何使用词语。

维特根斯坦还论证了私人语言*——只能被一个人所理解的语言——是不可能的。因此语言不能从具体某个人的内在思维中获得意义，因为意义并非私人的思想状态。语言依赖于公众的使用而获得意义。

《哲学研究》拒斥抽象之物，强调人类语境的重要性。维特根斯坦认为，哲学问题若脱离其所产生的人类处境，则是不可理解的。要理解抽象的哲学思想，如真理与意义，我们需要考察人们的实际生活。

该著作目前仍然被广泛地研究与讨论，它无疑是 20 世纪最具影响的哲学著作之一。然而，鲜有人会声称彻底读懂了这本书。阐释者们一直争论它究竟说了些什么，而哲学家与其他读者们则会继续从中发现新的洞见与思想。

《哲学研究》的学术价值

《哲学研究》一书艰涩难懂，一来因为它涉及的问题困难而复杂，二来因为维特根斯坦非同寻常的写作方式。他并不是提出论题并直截了当地加以论证，而是围绕着这些论题进行一番评论与例证。因此,即使该书的单个部分常常清楚易读,但要看出这些部分的总体关联,则非易事。

不管怎么说,《哲学研究》一书读起来还是愉快的。维特根斯坦的文笔很好,所以这本书能当作文学作品来欣赏。书中充满了有趣的想法、隐喻和暗示。例如,维特根斯坦将我们使用语言的方式比喻为玩游戏,这一观点影响了许多读者,他们发现这本书使自己悟到了新的思维方法。维特根斯坦在该书序言中自道,其目标为激发读者独立思考。

该书与许多学科都有关联。它无疑是一部革命性的哲学著作,但也对诸多别的领域产生了影响。它强调社会环境对语言的塑造,这一观点对语言学家来说是十分重要的。此外,维特根斯坦还认为我们是用语言来做事而非陈述真理的,这一观点影响了神学家*与文学批评家。例如,神学家感兴趣的不仅是宗教语言如何陈述关于上帝的假定事实,还有其如何表达情感。

《哲学研究》的影响也波及学术界之外,激发了作家、诗人,及电影制片人的灵感,其中包括艾弗·阿姆斯特朗·理查兹*、德里克·贾曼*和戴维·福斯特·华莱士*。其原因是维特根斯坦强调日常生活、语言,以及社会与文化间差异的重要性。该书影响至今不衰,因为相比于维特根斯坦之前的作家,我们在当今更能意识到文化差异的重要性。

该书也提供了一种能让读者从中受益的方法。维特根斯坦处理难题的方式是寻找新的方法来考察它们。他相信解决问题的最佳方式是对其做出正确的阐述。通常,一旦我们明白该怎样发问,那么找到问题的答案就容易多了。假如以我们询问"请"这个词的含义为例,如果我们去寻找该词代表的唯一含义,那么就会走入死胡同。取而代之的是，我们应该去考察该词是如何使用的。我们说"请"是为了获得什么东西，或是为了礼貌等等。

　　维特根斯坦认为，哲学问题源于我们使用语言的方式。因此，如果能够澄清我们使用的词句，那么我们就能够将这个世界看得更加清楚。维特根斯坦相信哲学问题本质上就是语言的混乱。这是一个有争议的观点。哲学问题在多大程度上是语言问题呢？但不论如何，维特根斯坦解决问题的方法，即通过考察我们描述问题的方式来解决问题，是行之有效的。

---

1. 路德维希·维特根斯坦：《逻辑哲学论》，D. F. 皮尔斯和 B. F. 麦吉尼斯译，伦敦：劳特利奇出版社，1974 年。

第一部分：学术渊源

1 作者生平与历史背景

要点

- 《哲学研究》是 20 世纪最重要的哲学著作之一,它影响了我们思考语言、心灵与哲学的方式。
- 维特根斯坦熟悉英德两国其同时代的一些最重要的思想家。在研读他们的著作时,他也是一位特立独行的思想家,会将他人的与自己的观点详加审视。
- 维特根斯坦写了两部伟大的哲学著作:《逻辑哲学论》和《哲学研究》。《哲学研究》对《逻辑哲学论》中的思想进行了深刻批判。

为何要读这部著作?

《哲学研究》出版于 1953 年,它是 20 世纪最重要的哲学著作之一,也是维特根斯坦对其思想的最终的、权威的陈述。年轻时,维特根斯坦在《逻辑哲学论》一书中曾提出大胆而独创的哲学观点。但多年之后,他彻底改变了先前的观点,并在《哲学研究》一书中提出了一种迥然不同的哲学方法。

维特根斯坦在该书中探讨了语言、人类的心智以及哲学的本质等一系列哲学核心问题,他对每个问题的观点一直是人们讨论的对象。不论在哪种情况下,他都建议我们密切关注人类身处的现实处境;此外,他也强调应对细节做细致入微的观察,而不要去建构庞大的理论。他并未去创建一种理论以揭示词是如何成为对象之名的,而是认为我们应该考察名称在日常言谈中的**实际使用**。

维特根斯坦在语言哲学与心灵哲学中采用的方法影响很大。具有同样影响力的是他对哲学本身的态度。维特根斯坦将哲学问题归因于语言使用的混乱或盲目,他相信这些问题的解决之道乃澄清语言的使用。

> "路德维希·维特根斯坦身上散发着一种独特的魅力,他对21世纪哲学的发展所产生的巨大影响也不足以解释这种魅力。即便那些不关心分析哲学的人也对他十分推崇。人们写了很多关于他的诗歌,很多绘画都从他那里获得了灵感,他的作品还被谱成了乐曲。"
> ——瑞·蒙克:《维特根斯坦传:天才之为责任》

作者生平

维特根斯坦1889年生于奥地利维也纳一个豪富的实业家家庭。其家庭成员具有很高的文化修养,特别在音乐方面。其兄保罗·维特根斯坦是一位成功的钢琴演奏家,家庭的其他几位成员也颇有音乐天赋,其中也包括维特根斯坦本人,不过他的欣赏品味有些老派。他对莫扎特*、贝多芬*、舒伯特*这类德国与奥地利的古典传统抱有热情,而对他那个时代的音乐则有些鄙夷。[1]

维特根斯坦遵照他父亲的意愿,去了英格兰的曼彻斯特大学学习工程学,在那里,他对逻辑与数学哲学产生了兴趣。1911年,他未等取得学位便离开了曼彻斯特,赴剑桥大学在伯特兰·罗素这位杰出的哲学家与逻辑学家*(研究逻辑的人)门下学习。罗素曾写过一本关于数学基础的重要著作,叫《数学原则》[2],维特根斯坦读过此书,并非常欣赏。

第一次世界大战爆发后,维特根斯坦离开了剑桥,加入了奥地利军队。从军期间他撰写了早期代表作《逻辑哲学论》。该书于

1921年首次出版，它提出了一种普遍的语言理论，揭示了词句是如何获得意义的。维特根斯坦相信，哲学问题产生于意义与语言的问题，《逻辑哲学论》揭示了这类问题的解决之道。他认为自己在这部著作中已解决了哲学的主要问题，因此放弃了哲学，在奥地利当了一名小学教员。

与此同时，《逻辑哲学论》不论在英格兰还是在欧洲都产生了巨大的影响。维特根斯坦1929年重返剑桥时，他已享有盛名，被认为是一位挑战既定信念的有创见的思想家。然而，他已彻底改变了写《逻辑哲学论》时的那些观点。尽管没有人能肯定，然而这也许正是他重返剑桥，重拾哲学的原因——他相信自己还有未竟之业。在剑桥，他就逻辑、语言哲学、心智哲学及数学哲学所做的讲座和哲学讨论，吸引了大批学生，他们渴望理解并发展他的思想。在其有生之年，维特根斯坦的思想通过口耳相传，或其讲座笔记和手稿的私下传播才得以扩散。这些笔记和手稿为《哲学研究》的形成打下了基础。

维特根斯坦自1929年起在剑桥大学以教师与学者的身份工作，直至1951年他62岁去世时。在那里，他逐渐形成了支撑《哲学研究》的大部分思想，并在挪威和爱尔兰幽居期间撰写了其中一部分。[3] 我们现在看到的这本书的内容，大部分是在1936年到1949年期间完成的。

创作背景

维特根斯坦年轻时，维也纳是一个文化创造力勃发的城市。西格蒙德·弗洛伊德*的心理分析理论（即通过让患者谈论他的梦、感觉与记忆来治疗其情感与心理问题）、阿诺尔德·勋伯格*的音乐以及古斯塔夫·克林姆特*的艺术都于20世纪初在此兴起。虽然维特根斯坦不喜欢与传统格格不入的现代主义*音乐，但维也纳富有创新精神的文化环境毕竟影响了他，使他对弗洛伊德的理论抱有浓厚兴趣。维也纳的昆德曼巷有一座房子，是维特根斯坦为他姐姐设计的，这件建筑作品彰显了现代主义的影响。

在《哲学研究》一书的序言中，维特根斯坦提到了"时代的黑暗"。[4]该序是在1945年1月写的，因此很多读者猜测他在影射第二次世界大战。然而，传记作家瑞·蒙克却指出，维特根斯坦其实是在影射当时的文化环境——尤其是自然科学的一手遮天。[5]虽然维特根斯坦对科学既熟悉又感兴趣，到了写作《哲学研究》时，他开始认识到科学理性的重要性被夸大到了危险的地步。他的后期著作可视为对今天所谓的"唯科学主义"*（认为科学是认识世界的唯一重要方式）的预先反驳。

---

1. 瑞·蒙克：《维特根斯坦传：天才之为责任》，伦敦：温特吉出版社，1991年，第13页。
2. 伯特兰·罗素：《数学原理》，伦敦：艾伦与休恩出版社，1903年。
3. 蒙克：《维特根斯坦传》，第361及之后几页、第520及之后几页。
4. 路德维希·维特根斯坦：《哲学研究》，伊丽莎白·安斯康姆译，牛津：布莱克威尔出版社，2001年。
5. 蒙克：《维特根斯坦传》，第486页。

2 学术背景

要点

- 许多现代哲学家，尤其自伊曼努尔·康德*以来，都关注于对人类思维的范围与本质的认识。
- 20世纪早期，戈特洛布·弗雷格、伯特兰·罗素等哲学家开始相信，研究人类思维的最佳方式乃研究语言。
- 在语言的重要性这点上，维特根斯坦与弗雷格和罗素的观点是一致的，但他强调的是语言的各种不同的用法。

著作语境

18世纪后期，德国伟大的哲学家伊曼努尔·康德提出了一种新的哲学方法，这种方法在20世纪及之后仍发挥着影响。康德考察哲学问题的方式是探寻人类心灵与思维的结构如何影响我们对世界的理解。他相信，研究我们思考世界的方式能阐明关于真理、意义与知识的传统哲学问题。

康德称他的方法为"哥白尼式的转向"。哥白尼*是一位伟大的数学家与天文学家，他颠覆了人们对于太阳系的传统认识，从而为16世纪早期的文艺复兴*思想带来了变革。他提出地球是围绕太阳运转的，这一观点取代了太阳围绕地球运转的成见。同样，康德也相信，通过假定知识是由人脑的构造，而非我们周围世界的结构塑造的，我们才能解释人类的知识。

康德的计划是理解人类知识与理性的限度，因为那样我们才能了解为何一些哲学的核心命题从未得到解答。这类问题包括上帝是否存在，宇宙是否永恒。康德认为，这些问题都是不可回答的，因为他们企图在不可能有答案处寻找答案：欲回答超越人类理性界限的问题。

> "凭借弗雷格，哲学的真正对象才最终得以确立：也就是说，首先，哲学的目标是分析**思想**的结构；其次，对思想的研究必须与对**思维**的心理过程的研究截然区分开来；最后，分析思想的唯一恰当的方法乃分析**语言**。"
> ——迈克尔·达米特：《真理及其他难解之谜》

学科概览

20世纪，哲学家们以语言学的方式来阐释康德的问题。他们发现思维的界限与语言的界限存在直接的联系，两者的界限也就是语词表达的界限。于是，他们开始将语言问题视为哲学的中心问题。

维特根斯坦撰写《哲学研究》之际，所谓的"分析哲学"*的发展早已引起了英语世界哲学的变革。这一哲学流派关注逻辑，注重对语言的精密分析，并对科学充满敬意。

分析哲学发展过程中的一位核心人物是德国哲学家与数学家戈特洛布·弗雷格，他在1884年出版了《算术基础》一书。[1] 弗雷格为语言哲学做出了巨大的贡献。他旨在通过考察表述思想的语言来分析思想。但与维特根斯坦不同的是，他的分析面向的是语言在科学与数学上的使用。

还有一位重要人物，即与维特根斯坦亦师亦友的英国哲学家、逻辑学家伯特兰·罗素。罗素将语言的主要目的视为提供对世界的精确表征。他认为，如果能将语言打造得更为精准，那么世界也会得到更好的表征。他运用了现代逻辑的工具来达到这一目标。罗素在其影响深远的著作，包括《论指称》[2]，以及与阿尔弗雷德·诺斯·怀特海[m]合著的多卷本数学逻辑著作《数学原理》中阐述了他的这些观点。[3]

学术渊源

很难确切知道究竟哪些哲学家影响过维特根斯坦，因为他通常不引用别人的观点，也不按惯例列出参考文献。不过他确实提到过戈特洛布·弗雷格对他的深刻影响。理解《哲学研究》的一条路径是将其视为对弗雷格哲学的修正，它将关注点从语言的科学使用扩展到了语言的非科学使用。

在剑桥大学的最初几年（1911—1914），维特根斯坦拜罗素为师，并开始对罗素产生了众所周知的影响。然而，到了1936年维特根斯坦动笔撰写《哲学研究》之时，两位哲学家已不再是密友，也鲜有私人来往了。维特根斯坦不喜欢那个时期罗素撰写的通俗的、缺乏技术含量的作品。罗素也同样不喜欢维特根斯坦的后期著作，不过他对他的这位学生仍有重要影响。两人的区别在于，罗素认为语言的目的是对现实进行表象——形成一种世界的图像——而维特根斯坦强调的则是语言多种多样的用途。此外，罗素认为语言应该提炼，应该被打造得更加精确，而维特根斯坦则坚持认为日常语言本身已足够用了。

在很多方面，《哲学研究》与20世纪30年代哲学舞台上最重要的运动是背道而驰的，即深受弗雷格、罗素及早期维特根斯坦本人影响的运动：逻辑实证主义[*]。它是由一群被称为"维也纳小组"的奥地利与德国的哲学家发起的，其中最为重要的人物是鲁道夫·卡尔纳普*，它强调对语言进行逻辑分析。这群哲学家都是经验主义*者，他们相信人类的所有知识都来自经验。他们认为，只有能够在经验中得到验证的句子——能被实验和观察证实——才具有意义。

因此，例如询问日本现在几点钟是**有**意义的，因为这是可以核实的。然而，如果去问上帝是否善良，或莫扎特与贝多芬这两位作曲家谁更优秀，则是**没有**意义的，因为这类事情（在逻辑实证主义者看来）既不能证实也不能推翻。以此为基础，他们指责许多传统的关于哲学、伦理、宗教与艺术的谈话是毫无意义的。

而维特根斯坦却对此持不同观点。他认为语言的科学使用仅仅是语言的诸多用法之一，因此，并不像逻辑实证主义者设想的那样，判断何物具有意义的统一方法其实并不存在。

---

1. 戈特洛布·弗雷格：《算术基础》，J. L. 奥斯汀译，牛津：布莱克威尔出版社，1950 年。
2. 伯特兰·罗素："论指称"，《心灵》1905 年第 14 卷：第 479—493 页。
3. 伯特兰·罗素和 A. N. 怀特海：《数学原理》，剑桥：剑桥大学出版社，1910—1913 年。

3 主导命题

要点

- 哲学家感兴趣的问题是：词句是如何获得意义的？
- 弗雷格从真理入手理解意义：他认为一个句子的意义是由其为真的条件赋予的。而逻辑实证主义者认为一个句子的意义是由我们判断其真假的方式提供的。
- 维特根斯坦反对用单一的方法分析语言。他说，我们应该考察语言的各种用法，以此来了解语言的本质。

核心问题

维特根斯坦在撰写《哲学研究》时从不对我们清楚地陈述他的意图，因此很难确认该书拟解答的核心问题究竟是哪个。不过要理解这本书倒有个有效的方法，即认为它是在回答如下问题：我们的词句是如何获得意义的？该问题对于维特根斯坦之前的哲学家来说也至关重要。

不过，该书还回答了一个更大的问题：我们的心灵状态——我们的信念、欲望、期待、记忆等——是如何获得意义的？在该问题中，"意义"一词具有不同（但也相关）的含义。该问题关注的是哲学家所谓的上述心灵状态的"意向性"*，或者说这些心灵状态是如何指向事物的。比方说，欲望是如何**指向**某个具体事物的？我对冰激凌的欲望又如何成为对某份冰激凌的欲望的？

这些也许是就语言与心灵能问的最根本的问题了。由于自然科学的成功，这些问题在现代变得尤为紧迫。比方说，科学家能依照诸如动物的行为更好地解释世界，而人类的行为却难以用科学的方式加以解释，这正是因为其中很大一部分涉及意义与意图。因此，意义的本质就成为一个亟待回答的知性问题。

> "该学派的目标不及过去大多数哲学家的目标那样宏大，但它所取得的一些成就却像科学家的成就那样牢靠。"
> ——伯特兰·罗素：《西方哲学史》

参与者

对维特根斯坦影响最大的是弗雷格，他致力于构造一种语义*理论——即有关语言意义的理论。他主张"意义的单位"是思想，思想的意义在于其"真值条件"，或者说是思想为真实世界的必然存在方式。

罗素在《逻辑原子论哲学》一书[1]中采纳了弗雷格的思想，这本书是在他1918年的讲座的基础上形成的。在该书中，罗素解释了我们对世界的言说与思想是如何获得意义的。在他看来，我们之所以能够对世界进行思考，是因为我们的心灵表象了世界中的事态（表象主义*）。心灵状态与实际事态间的表象关系是一个基点：它解释了我们可拥有的关于世界的多种多样的思想。因此，当我说"猫在椅子上"，那么我就给出了一个关于世界的表象。如果猫**是**在椅子上，那么我说的便是真的；如果猫不在椅子上，那么我说的便是假的。不论哪种情况，我都对猫在椅子上进行了表象。

维特根斯坦在《逻辑哲学论》中也同意这一观点，但之后他却开始相信这仅仅是语言诸多用法中的一种。因此，当我说"我累了"的时候，我可能仅仅在告诉你我的感受；但我也可能想让你去沏杯茶，我好放松一下。在这种情况下，我说"我累了"的真正原因根本不是对世界进行表象，而是影响你的行为。

罗素相信，通过将思想分析为其构件（逻辑原子主义*），我们就能发现思想是如何与世界勾连在一起的。如果这么做，我们就会发现这些构件是些私有的知觉与经验——罗素称之为"感觉材料"*。最终，我们只能将感觉材料称为构件，因为我们只能与感觉材料有知觉上的接触。

20世纪三四十年代，正值维特根斯坦逐渐形成《哲学研究》中的思想之际，当时最为蓬勃的哲学运动——逻辑实证主义日益主导了哲学争论。像弗雷格与罗素一样，逻辑实证主义者关注的是语义。他们相信，哲学的任务是探寻语句的准确分析，从而发现其真正的含义。这的确曾是判断语句是否有意义的唯一途径。

逻辑实证主义者提出了一个理论，认为只有能够在经验中得以验证的句子——能被实验或观察证实——才算具有意义。因此，诸如抽象的、宗教的，或者形而上学*的（何为根本之**存在**）讨论实际上是无意义的。就以"乞力马扎罗山顶有朵雏菊"这句话为例，你能去乞力马扎罗山顶看看是否真的有朵雏菊，这样便能检验这句话的真假。然而，像"上帝爱我们"这类句子是不可能检验其真假的。因此在逻辑实证主义者看来，这句话毫无意义。

当代论战

在《哲学研究》一书中，维特根斯坦反驳了弗雷格、罗素及逻辑实证主义者的许多观点。他在引用他人观点时几乎不提对方的名字，不过弗雷格与罗素（他之前的老师）是极少的几个例外。在

《哲学研究》的主要段落中,维特根斯坦很明显是在回应罗素,虽然没有指名道姓。[2]

维特根斯坦说道,我们应当关注语言的使用,而非脱离语境的词句。他鼓励我们考察"语言游戏"*:即人们为特定目的而使用语言的具体情境。这包含了弗雷格与逻辑实证主义者们所关注的语言在科学中的使用。更易引起争议的是,维特根斯坦将文学与宗教上的语言使用也包括了进来,这可是被逻辑实证主义者们驳斥为无意义的。

维特根斯坦否认对意义有统一的理解规则,对句子有唯一的正确分析。他相信我们能用不同的方式来分析思想,这取决于思考的目的。

例如,我们可以将"约翰是光棍"这句话解释成"约翰未婚",但第二句话并不比第一句更基础、更重要,只不过更有助于向不明白"光棍"一词者解释这句话的含义罢了。逻辑实证主义认为,哲学靠澄清语句的真实含义充当科学工作的助手。这种观点是难以成立的。

再想一下"我累了"这句话,它或许是对我感受的平心静气的报道,或许是想让你去帮我沏茶。两者截然不同,却用了同一句话来表达。关键在于:我是在两种不同的场合为不同的目的而使用同一句话的。既然在后期的维特根斯坦看来,意义即使用,那么具有意义的并非句子,而是言说它们的具体情境。假如我说"上帝爱我们",那么我可能在报道我看待上帝的方式,可能想要让你振作起来,也可能是在开玩笑。这些都是对同一句话的截然不同的用法。你不能问某一句话究竟有没有意义。因此,在维特根斯坦看来,逻辑实证主义是错误的。

维特根斯坦完全否定了罗素的观点，尤其是"表象"这个抽象概念。相反，他却认为，如果我们想要理解我们的思想并谈论这个世界，那么就应该考察一下我们在具体情境中的具体意图。语言的意义来自公共的环境，而非个人的经验。因此，维特根斯坦也否定了罗素的"感觉材料"这一概念。

尽管维特根斯坦驳斥了前人的观点，但对他们的观点却有着深刻的理解。他从现代逻辑与现代哲学中汲取了真正的教训，因此，《哲学研究》可视为对其同时代哲学家们的强有力的反驳。

---

1. 伯特兰·罗素：《逻辑原子论哲学》，伦敦：劳特利奇出版社，2009年。
2. 例如，札记79很明显是在影射罗素的摹状词理论，大致从札记243开始的对私人语言和内心经验的讨论则是在挑战罗素对于知觉的观点。

4 作者贡献

要点

- 维特根斯坦以"意义即使用"这句口号总结了他的观点。
- 维特根斯坦的观点使得对语言日常使用的分析,及语言在日常生活中的作用得到了新的重视。
- 维特根斯坦前辈的,甚至他自己的早期著作,常强调语言在**科学**中的使用才是至关重要的。而在《哲学研究》中,维特根斯坦则仅仅视科学为语言的诸多用法之一。

作者目标

维特根斯坦曾将其目标描述为使人们"改变他们的思维方式"。[1] 在《哲学研究》一书中,其意图与其说是说服人们相信存在某种哲学指导原则,不如说是揭示普遍的错误与混乱的根源。维特根斯坦尤其想引导我们摆脱关于语言与心灵的宽泛的、普遍的理论,并鼓励我们关注具体的细节。[2] 他说,哲学不同于物理学与生物学,无须形成这类普遍的理论,因为哲学的研究对象是难以理解的。进一步说,我们思考与言说世界的日常方式已经很完善了。只有当我们误用已经在我们手上的工具时,哲学问题才会产生。说得极端点,若维特根斯坦的目标实现了,那么哲学问题便消失了,哲学家便不得不保持沉默。

有些评论者[3]相信,维特根斯坦认为哲学的目的应该是阻止坏的思想,而不是达至真理。他们说,维特根斯坦将从事哲学当成一种治疗*,他仅仅旨在消除知性上的问题与混乱。不过,《哲学研究》一书也确实包含了对于语言哲学、心灵哲学和数学哲学的许多传统问题的见解。其方法当然是反对建构理论的，但也对积极的哲学思考具有贡献。

维特根斯坦的目标影响了他的写作方式。他的语气是对话式的，书的结构也不是传统的书面论辩所采用的。首先出现的声音代表维特根斯坦想要反驳的那类哲学方法，接着，他再用自己的声音予以答复。这种非同寻常的结构让人难以阐释维特根斯坦的意图。因此，当前对该书的争论不仅针对书中的那些论点，还针对如何才能最好地理解维特根斯坦提出这些论点的意图。

> "就使用'意义'一词的情境的一个大类而言——尽管不是所有情境——该词可定义为：一个词的意义就是它在语言中的使用。"
>
> ——路德维希·维特根斯坦:《哲学研究》

研究方法

维特根斯坦处理语言的方法强调说话者对词句的具体使用。为了理解语言的运作，他发明了"语言游戏"这一概念。一种语言游戏即为某个具体目的而使用语言的一种情境。游戏中的各种招数即说话者所用的语词，正如在棋类游戏中，特定的规则指导着棋子的走动。

例如，在《哲学研究》开篇，维特根斯坦描绘了一种人们建造房子的语言游戏。一位建筑工人喊出"板石""柱石"等词，他的助手则取来对应的那样东西。维特根斯坦认为，如果我们要问"板石"一词对建筑工人来说**是什么意思**，我们就得描述一下他们拿这些词来干什么。

维特根斯坦相信，一个人说着某种语言，比如英语，就玩着各种各样的语言游戏，一个特定的词的用法依赖于具体的场景。语言的使用从总体上来说，并不受任何明确的规则的支配，而是依赖各种具体的场景。因此，为了理解说话者正在某个具体场合干什么，我们就须理解他们正在玩什么语言游戏。

在维特根斯坦看来，上述方法得出的一个结论是，科学家所玩的仅仅是诸多语言游戏之一种。若将语言的使用作为一个整体来理解，那么其科学的使用并不具有特殊地位，维特根斯坦也远不如其前辈那样强调语言的科学用法。

时代贡献

尽管维特根斯坦批评了其同辈哲学家弗雷格与罗素的观点，但也从他们身上获益匪浅。看待其工作的方式之一，即将之视为对弗雷格与罗素的思想的深化与扩展。后两者关注的是科学语言的使用，而维特根斯坦扩展了这一论题，使之涵盖了我们用语言所做的其他事情。

维特根斯坦对之前学派的哲学思想的批评，也能在他那个年代的其他著作中找到共鸣。比如，在他与"日常语言哲学*家"之间就能找到一些相似之处。这一学派基本上是以牛津大学为阵营的，约翰·郎肖·奥斯汀*是其中一名成员，他也坚信哲学应当澄清语言上的混乱，并认为理解语言的最好方式是考察普通说话者对语词的使用。与奥斯汀和维特根斯坦一样，吉尔伯特·赖尔*也仔细考察了语言的使用，在强调行为的重要性这点上，他同维特根斯坦的意见也是一致的。如果我们想要理解心理状态的本质，拿愤怒来说，那么我们就应当考察一下愤怒之人有哪些行为。

然而，对于维特根斯坦的思想，虽然赖尔是有共鸣的，但奥斯汀起先并不能理解。或许这正是因为维特根斯坦未按常规方式来呈现其思想的缘故吧：未遵循传统学术讨论的套路，而是提供了一系列札记、阐释与例子。总而言之，维特根斯坦对于逻辑实证主义、对于该流派以逻辑为基础的语言分析以及对于主流分析哲学的批判较之奥斯汀、赖尔等人更为彻底、更具挑战性。这就意味着，维特根斯坦的作品等待了更长时日才被纳入学术主流之中。

---

1. 路德维希·维特根斯坦：《关于美学的讲座与谈话》，牛津：布莱克威尔出版社，1967年，札记28。
2. 路德维希·维特根斯坦：《哲学研究》，伊丽莎白·安斯康姆译，牛津：布莱克威尔出版社，2001年，札记109。
3. 尤其参见鲁珀特·里德和艾丽斯·克拉里编写的《维特根斯坦新论》（伦敦：劳特利奇出版社，2000年）中的一些文章。

第二部分：学术思想

5 思想主脉

要点

- 按《哲学研究》一书的观点,一个词的意义取决于它在语言中的使用。因此,为了理解词句的意义,我们需要考察它们在具体情境中的使用。
- 对语言的理解基于至少可被一部分人观察到的对象和行为。语词的意义不由纯粹私有的感觉决定。
- 维特根斯坦没有以一整篇连贯的论证来呈现其思想,而是提供了大量彼此相关的札记,它们揭示了他所讨论的主题间存在诸多关联。

核心主题

维特根斯坦的《哲学研究》一书包含了若干主导论题。第一个是**意义**在**使用**中才能被最好地理解的思想;第二个是有关规则与如何遵循规则的讨论;第三个是对于"私人语言"*——只能被一个人理解的语言——的反驳。

该著作以维特根斯坦的语言与意义观开场,[1] 一开场他便提出,一个辞句的意义来自它在人类生活中的使用。他写道,"就使用'意义'一词的情境的一个**大**类而言——尽管不是所有情境——该词可定义为:一个词的意义就是它在语言中的使用。"[2] 他尤其驳斥这样的观点,即事物与人的名称之所以具有意义,靠的仅仅是将名称与对象一一绑定。

接着,维特根斯坦讨论了规则的遵循。[3] 他主张遵循一项特定的规则并非只是正确地阐释一个具体的词的含义（例如，在一项正确使用某词的规则中，"光棍"一词仅用来指未婚成年男性）。他认为，遵循规则即在如何言说与行动方面与他人达成一致意见。

再接下来讨论的是"私人语言的论证"。[4] 维特根斯坦论述道，像"疼痛"这类描写心灵状态的语词的意义并非通过说话者个人的——即私有的——经验获得，这些经验只有说话者自己理解。相反，跟其他词一样，"疼痛"一词的意义是在与他人的交流与共同的使用中获得的。

> "我所能写的最好的东西，无非也就是些哲学札记了；如果我违背自己思想的自然趋向，试图往单一的方向上推进它们，那么它们马上就会一瘸一拐起来。这固然与这项研究的本质有关。因为它迫使我们在一片广袤的思想之域纵横穿行。本书中的那些哲学札记，可以说，正如在这些漫长而错综的旅途中所作的许多幅风景速写。"
>
> ——路德维希·维特根斯坦：《哲学研究》

思想探究

维特根斯坦指向的是语言的广泛使用。他坚持认为，只有依照人们的具体目的与他们的生活环境，语言与行为才能为我们所理解。语言的使用即维特根斯坦所谓的"生活形式"[5] 的一部分。

像英语、法语等语言，它们不仅仅交流思想，也展现了讲英语与法语者的态度与生活方式。比如在"谢天谢地""为了上帝的更大荣耀"这类表述中，说话者表达的是某种生活态度。要是听话者不理解这些表述，我们光凭告诉他们上帝是谁是解释不清的。这或许是因为他们的文化太与众不同，以至理解不了其中所表达的**态度**。

维特根斯坦写道,假如狮子能讲话,我们也理解不了它。[6] 为什么呢?并不是我们跟狮子不能谈论相同的事物,很可能我们都有称呼羚羊与山的词汇,但这还不足以产生理解,因为狮子有着迥然不同的生活方式与世界观。简言之,我们彼此的生活形式不同。

维特根斯坦相信,我们应当考察语言在特定情境中的使用,这便是他所谓的"语言游戏",在其中,词句依照特定的规则并为具体的目的而使用。

他认为,只有考察语言游戏,我们才能理解词句的正确与错误使用的差别。然而,这确实会引起以下问题:是什么支配了语言在未来的正确与错误的使用呢?

维特根斯坦坚持认为,任何词句在过去的使用都不足以决定其在将来的使用。为了适应新的需要,总会有不同的方式来解释过去的用法。

总而言之,语词使用的任何规则都不可能强大到足以决定新情境中所谓"正确"的运用。规则总能被重新解释,因此,描述未来种种行为的方式,便是使其适应现存的规则。维特根斯坦写道,"没有一条规则能决定行动方式,因为每一种行动方式都能改变去适应规则。"[7] 一旦情境改变,我们往往需要重新决定如何使用语言。

维特根斯坦将同样的结论也推广到了私有心灵实体*——观念、思想、感觉——就和抽象规则一样:它们都不能支配语言的使用。心灵上的表征可被认为是在头脑中,而非在纸上形成的规则,像上述规则一样,它们也能被重新解释,以适应未来的种种运用。

再概括点说,维特根斯坦反驳的是这样一种观点,即认为任何语言都能从个人的内心私生活中获得意义。我们倾向于认为,我们用以描述感觉与感受的语言是个人的。例如，**我**所使用的"疼痛"一词是从**我**对疼痛的私人感受中获得意义的。然而，维特根斯坦坚信没有一个词是这样运作的。语词的正确与否必须以公共标准来判断，而不能依赖私人经验。不然，就没有办法来检验其使用正确与否了。

语言表述

《哲学研究》是一部写得颇为好看的书，很有文学性。它的行文没有那么刻板，语言明白晓畅，且几乎没有专业术语。因此，它读起来是相当有趣的。

不过，这并不是说它容易理解。其中一部分原因是维特根斯坦并未清楚地陈述他的思想与观点。相反，他允许他的思想与观点在涵盖诸多领域的广泛讨论中生长。他在该书序言中写道，这项研究的本质意味着读者必须"在一片广袤的思想之域纵横穿行。"[8]

因此，我们很难将该书归入传统的学院派哲学中。不同的读者都能对它做出不同的解释；此外，要发现维特根斯坦与其他哲学家在思想上的交集也是相当困难的。

对于维特根斯坦的写作风格，有两种截然不同的观点。有些评论者——如英国哲学家迈克尔·达米特*——提出，该书的风格是由维特根斯坦的个性，而非其所写的内容造成的。他们推想维特根斯坦的观点也能用更为传统的哲学形式表达，并以条理清晰的论证来支撑。[9] 而另一些人，如美国哲学家斯坦利·卡维尔*，则坚持认为《哲学研究》一书的风格对其内容是至关重要的。[10] 卡维尔说，维特根斯坦的目标之一是试图阐明普遍的理论会导致错误与混乱，我们只有通过对具体情况的细心思考才能得出清晰的语言观。

1. 路德维希·维特根斯坦：《哲学研究》，伊丽莎白·安斯康姆译，牛津：布莱克威尔出版社，2001年，札记1—184。
2. 维特根斯坦：《哲学研究》，札记43。
3. 维特根斯坦：《哲学研究》，札记185—242。
4. 维特根斯坦：《哲学研究》，札记243—363。
5. 维特根斯坦：《哲学研究》，札记19、241。
6. 维特根斯坦：《哲学研究》，札记223。
7. 维特根斯坦：《哲学研究》，札记201。
8. 维特根斯坦：《哲学研究》，第vii页。
9. 例如，可参见迈克尔·达米特《真理及其他难解之谜》（伦敦：达克沃斯出版社，1978年）一书中"维特根斯坦的数学哲学"一文。
10. 斯坦利·卡维尔：《理性的诉求》，牛津：牛津大学出版社，1979年，第xx页。

6 思想支脉

要点

- 维特根斯坦相信,哲学不应力图去获得新的知识,而应解决因思维混乱而产生的思想混乱。
- "面相知觉"*即我们以不同方式听见或看见事物的经验。维特根斯坦运用这类经验来探讨知觉与思维之间的关系。
- 维特根斯坦的思想已被人们广泛研究,但哲学家们尚未完全接受他的思想。

其他思想

《哲学研究》一书涉及范围很广,探讨了多个主题。它还包含了如下副主题:维特根斯坦对哲学的理解;他对概念分析*(对语词与概念进行分析以探寻其意义)的批评;以及他称之为"面相知觉"*的概念(同样的对象如何能以不同的方式来观察)。"面相知觉"这一概念也可称作"视为"。

维特根斯坦在书中写道,"语言休假时,哲学问题就产生了。"[1] 他认为,当我们以不恰当的方式使用语言时,哲学上的混乱便产生了。某个特定的词或短语若按其固有的、自然的方式使用,是不会有什么问题的,问题在于其使用超出了正常的语境。他想象某人问道:"太阳上现在几点钟了?"[2] 此问题是没有确切答案的,但这并非因为询问正常环境中的时间有什么模糊不清之处。

概念分析的方法对于维特根斯坦的至近前辈,如罗素与逻辑实证主义者来说是十分重要的。概念分析以通过考察词句来分析其真实含义的方式对语言进行研究。维特根斯坦认为这一方法是有问题的：一个特定的句子并不存在唯一正确的分析。

该书的第二部分关注的是心理哲学*，不过维特根斯坦并没有想为出版而审读过这个部分。有些评论者，包括英国哲学家彼得·哈克*在内都认为这部分不应包含在《哲学研究》之内。这部分最著名的几个段落考察的是面相知觉——格式塔学派*心理学家曾研究过这种经验，例如，一个人在同一个形状中看出了两种不同的形象——这涉及知觉与思维的关系。

维特根斯坦以一幅图为例，这幅图看起来既像画了一只鸭子，又像画了一只兔子。如果你久久地盯着这幅图看，它好像反复地在鸭子图和兔子图之间切换。这种"面相切换"十分有趣，因为它们既能被解释为看见了新东西，也能被解释为获得了新思想，以至于思想与知觉似乎重叠了。维特根斯坦写道，"因此，在我们面前闪现的面相一半像视觉经验，一半像思想。"3

> "你的哲学目标是什么？为苍蝇飞出捕蝇瓶指明一条出路。"
>
> ——路德维希·维特根斯坦：《哲学研究》

思想探究

维特根斯坦对概念分析进行了清晰而坚定的批判。这是读者在该书中能明确辨识的论题之一。不过，他对分析这一概念的批判是明确针对罗素的，罗素将概念分析视为哲学的主要目标之一。这样一来，对于不熟悉罗素著作的读者而言，要理解维特根斯坦的观点就变得困难了。

维特根斯坦阐述了他对概念分析这一方法的见解,但他也提出了另一种方法,即语言游戏:想象人们为特定目的而使用语言的场景,这些目的虽跟我们的不同,但也能为我们的目的提供阐释。于是,关注的焦点便从词句转向了具体的话语与语言的使用。

想象这样的场景:在两个都在下雨的国家各有一人,两人都说了一句"在下雨"。句子是同样的句子,但也是两句言说动机不同的话。一个人可能是在告诉某人带上伞;而另一个人可能是在闲聊。维特根斯坦的观点是:具体语境创造了意义。

维特根斯坦未对语言游戏这一方法下过一个明确的定义,而是提供了大量语言游戏的例子。他规劝我们"不要想,而要看!"[4] 在这里,维特根斯坦充分施展了他的文学才华,生动描绘了各种场景。例如,他描绘了一个社群,那儿的语言是由像"板石""柱石"这类词的使用构成的,而他想象这个社群里的生活又是那么不同。[5] 维特根斯坦在构思这一场景中展示了惊人的想象力,因此,许多读者虽然对哲学方法不那么熟悉,但也能凭直觉把握《哲学研究》中的语言游戏方法。

在关于面相知觉的讨论中,维特根斯坦一再转回到一个问题,即一种面相经验是一个视觉问题还是一个思维问题。它似乎兼具两者的特征。一方面,虽然将鸭/兔解释为鸭子看似接近于具有一种思维;而另一方面,事实上这是一种视觉上的解释,这意味着它更像是**看见**一个新物体,或以一种新的方式观看同一个物体。

至于这些例子与《哲学研究》一书的其他论题有什么关系,人们的看法并不一致,不过维特根斯坦本人倒是给出了一个明晰的类比:正如人们观看图像一样,理解词句的方式亦是由语境以及听众的观点决定的。例如,一个说英语的人对"bank(银行/堤岸)"

一词的不同反应取决于该词究竟用来指一个金融机构，还是指一条河的堤岸。

被忽视之处

　　研究维特根斯坦《哲学研究》的论著已出版了不计其数。该文本的许多部分，或其论题的许多方面已不可能找到研究的空白了。不过，倒是仍有可能发现某些部分，它们具有不衰的哲学价值，但相对而言，并未引起人们重视。

　　尽管维特根斯坦的语言哲学已被广泛研究，不过仍有一些要素未被充分发掘。一个有趣的问题是，当代语言哲学和语言学理论能从维特根斯坦的方法中获得什么教益。最为重要的是语境在理解中所起的作用。讲某种语言的人是依靠语境因素和语言知识而达成相互理解的。对于我们相互理解至关重要的，是我们无疑过着人的生活这一事实："假如狮子能讲话"，维特根斯坦写道，"我们也理解不了它。"[6]

　　学者们以前可能忽视了这个观点，因为有些较有影响的对维特根斯坦语言观的阐释认为这一观点似乎是过时的。尤其是美国哲学家约翰·塞尔*，在专名问题上，他认为维特根斯坦是一名描写主义者——换言之，维特根斯坦相信一个名称的意义可用一组描述来确定。[7]例如，"摩西"这一名称的意义能够以诸如"率领以色列人走出埃及的那个人"等描述来确定。这一观点在近年来的哲学中不那么流行了，特别是自从美国哲学家与逻辑学家索尔·克里普克*出版了《命名与必然性》[8]一书以来。然而，也可以说维特根斯坦**不是**这个意义上的描写主义者，原因很简单，因为他反对所有的普遍理论。

1. 路德维希·维特根斯坦:《哲学研究》,伊丽莎白·安斯康姆译,牛津:布莱克威尔出版社,2001年,札记38。
2. 维特根斯坦:《哲学研究》,札记350。
3. 维特根斯坦:《哲学研究》,第168页。
4. 维特根斯坦:《哲学研究》,札记66。
5. 维特根斯坦:《哲学研究》,札记6。
6. 维特根斯坦:《哲学研究》,第190页。
7. 约翰·塞尔:"专名",《心灵》1958年第67卷:第166—173页。
8. 索尔·克里普克:《命名与必然性》,牛津:布莱克威尔出版社,1980年。

7 历史成就

要点

- 维特根斯坦启发了一种思考哲学本身、哲学与科学之关系的新方法。
- 最近几十年,出现了一种向形而上学*——对实在之构成的研究——以及在哲学中建立关于世界本质的理论的回归。于是,维特根斯坦的影响衰退了。
- 维特根斯坦的思想对哲学之外的许多学科也产生了影响。

观点评价

维特根斯坦启发了一种思考哲学本身以及哲学与科学之关系的新方法。他的哲学观至今仍有影响。在维特根斯坦看来,哲学并不构建关于世界的普遍理论,而应当以清除概念上的混乱为目标。

他区分科学与哲学的观点也同样具有影响。他相信两者具有不同的目标。科学的目标是获取关于世界的新知识,并构建理论对之进行解释。相比于科学,哲学贡献的并非知识,而是理解。通过哲学讨论,我们能够更好地理解我们的思想与观点。

有些评论家,其中最著名的或许是美国哲学家理查德·罗蒂*,认为维特根斯坦表明哲学已经终结。[1] 哲学已不再是一门知识性学科,以增长我们的知识为目标,这项工作现已交给科学来做了。尽管哲学渴望讨论关于善或人生意义等较为深奥的问题,但它已经被虚构文学取代了。这派思想的基础是对维特根斯坦**反驳**哲学中解释性理论的解读,但这一解读是有争议的。

> "一幅图像囚禁了我们。我们逃不出去,因为它在我们的语言之中,而语言似乎在执着地向我们重复着它。"
>
> ——路德维希·维特根斯坦:《哲学研究》

当时的成就

在哲学界,《哲学研究》一书的价值与意义从未达成过共识。有些哲学家[2]相信,该书给哲学带来了深刻的教益,只是尚未被充分接受与认识。他们特别引用了维特根斯坦的观点,即认为对语言的细致考察揭示了传统哲学对世界的形而上学的本质(即实在的基本元素)的探究是建立在混乱的基础上的。而另有些人[3]则认为该书是武断的、无说服力的。他们继续追问那些维特根斯坦认为无意义或误导性的传统哲学问题。

也许,《哲学研究》在今天的影响力的确不及20世纪50、60年代了。形而上学——这一研究构成实在的根本事物的哲学分支——在索尔·克里普克与戴维·刘易斯等哲学家的影响下再次流行了起来,而他们所采用的哲学方法又是与《哲学研究》的精神相违背的。维特根斯坦的哲学观——即有关我们看待世界的方式——已被建构关于世界本质的理论所取代。许多分析哲学家已不像20世纪中叶时他们的前辈那样,将语言问题当成哲学的中心问题。然而,这究竟是一时的潮流还是永久的事态,且让我们拭目以待吧。

维特根斯坦早期的影响大致局限于英国和北美。他的几位学生成为英美高校的学者,并在那里进行了对其著作的严谨探讨。[4]然而,别说在世界其他地方了,即便在欧洲大陆,维特根斯坦的著作也总是和英语国家的分析哲学这一狭小领域联系在一起。这一局面近年来有了改观,这得益于法国哲学家雅克·布弗莱斯*和阿兰·巴迪乌*等人的工作,以及人们对于探索维特根斯坦与其同时代德国哲学家马丁·海德格尔*著作之间联系的新兴趣。[5]

局限性

维特根斯坦的著作所产生的影响并不仅限于哲学领域,而是遍及了人文与社会科学。其中一个影响极为深远的领域是神学*。受《哲学研究》中的思想的影响,有些神学家已不再视宗教为一种形而上学的学说(一套被教导或信以为真的观念),或一种关于世界起源或本质的理论。[6]他们的关注点已经从宗教学说转移到了宗教实践——即某种宗教中实际发生了什么。更确切地说,维特根斯坦派的宗教学家坚信,宗教学说应当在宗教实践的语境下才能得到解释。从根本上讲,这是一场关于该如何理解宗教语言的争论,他们采纳了维特根斯坦的"意义即使用"这一观念:如果我们想理解宗教术语的意义,那么我们必须考察一下它们是如何使用的。

有些作者,其中最为著名的是加拿大哲学家卡伊·尼尔森*,将维特根斯坦的宗教观描述为"信仰主义"*。信仰主义认为宗教信仰建立在,或者说应当建立在信仰而非理性的基础上。然而,维特根斯坦派的宗教思想家,如戴维·菲利普*,则提出了反驳,认为这一描述是曲解。[7]维特根斯坦并未主张宗教信仰不能在哲学或科学的立场上予以批判。

社会学*与人类学*是维特根斯坦产生影响的其他两个领域——尤其是他对主体世界观的重要性的强调,该世界观旨在通过主体的视角及其亲身实践来描绘一个情境。

一个值得注意的例子便是科学社会学这一分支学科。该领域近年来有一个显著的趋势,即从各种科学观点自身出发来对它们进行考察。按此方法,从一个科学观点到另一个的转换,就不能被解释为朝着理论家所认定的真理的迈进。我们反倒应当凭过去的科学家**自己的**术语,即采用他们自己所采用的概念来理解他们的著作。早期热衷于这一方法的是托马斯·库恩*,他明确承认《科学革命的结构》[8]一书受了维特根斯坦的影响。一个更新的例子是戴维·布卢尔的著作,他是《维特根斯坦、规则与制度》[9]一书的作者。

维特根斯坦还对其他一些学科产生了影响,包括文学批评、艺术史、以及教育。[10]这些学科对维特根斯坦思想的应用已偏离了他在《哲学研究》中明确讨论的主题——偏离之严重,已让人无法确定维特根斯坦究竟会不会同意他们的观点。

---

1. 理查德·罗蒂:《哲学与自然之镜》,新泽西州普林斯顿:普林斯顿大学出版社,1979年。
2. 最近的例子可参见保罗·霍里奇:《维特根斯坦的元哲学》,牛津:牛津大学出版社,2013年;以及查尔斯·特拉维斯:《思想的基点》,牛津:牛津大学出版社,2006年。
3. 例如,可参见蒂莫西·威廉森:《哲学之哲学》,牛津:布莱克威尔出版社,2007年。
4. 较为重要的几位是康奈尔大学的诺曼·马尔科姆、牛津大学的伊丽莎白·安斯康姆以及伯明翰和利兹大学的彼得·吉奇。
5. 例如,可参见李·布雷弗:《无根据的根据:维特根斯坦与海德格尔研究》,马萨诸塞州剑桥:麻省理工学院出版社,2012年。
6. 例如,可参见弗格斯·克尔:《维特根斯坦之后的神学》,牛津:布莱克威尔出版社，1986 年。
7. 卡伊·尼尔森、D. Z. 菲利普：《维特根斯坦派的信仰主义？》，伦敦：SCM 出版社，2005 年。
8. 托马斯·库恩：《科学革命的结构》，芝加哥：芝加哥大学出版社，1962 年。
9. 戴维·布卢尔：《维特根斯坦、规则与制度》，伦敦：劳特利奇出版社，1997 年。
10. 例如，可参见詹姆斯·圭蒂：《维特根斯坦与文学经验的语法》，佐治亚州雅典：佐治亚大学出版社，1993 年。

8 著作地位

要点

- 维特根斯在他整个职业生涯中都关注语言与思维的关系。
- 《哲学研究》是其后期哲学的集大成之作，该书与其早期著作《逻辑哲学论》形成了对照。
- 《逻辑哲学论》与《哲学研究》是维特根斯坦最为著名、最被人广泛研究的著作，但或许后者对后来的思想家产生的影响最大。

定位

维特根斯坦的哲学生涯自然地分为两个主要阶段。从 1911 年到 1914 年，他在剑桥大学从事哲学研究。《逻辑哲学论》[1] 是一本薄薄的书，是他在一战前线和战争接近尾声时在意大利的蒙特卡西诺作战俘时写的。这本书表达了他的早期哲学思想。接着，他放弃了哲学，到奥地利乡村当了一名小学教员。直到 1929 年，他返回剑桥重操哲学旧业，并开启了一个新的阶段，这个阶段一直持续到他逝世。

《哲学研究》是维特根斯坦成熟期的关键著作，是他 1929 年至 1949 年这段时期研究的巅峰之作。他在 20 世纪 30 年代以来的其他手稿与评论也都出版了，它们揭示了他的思想是如何发展、完善，并最终体现在《哲学研究》这部书中的。[2]

维特根斯坦去世后，他的学生们编辑并出版了《哲学研究》一书。虽然维特根斯坦已将大部分手稿准备到了目前的样子，但也无法肯定他是否还会进一步修改。学者们在另一个问题上也莫衷一

是，即通常被称为《哲学研究》"第二部分"的那些内容究竟应视为该书的一部分，还是应视为一部独立的著作。³

从完成《哲学研究》后直到 1951 年去世的那几年里，维特根斯坦继续进行哲学写作。尽管他没有再写出整部的著作，但后来又出版了这一时期的几份打印稿，每种都是按主题组织起来的。最主要的两个主题是心理学哲学（该主题下所写的以《心理学哲学札记》为题出版）⁴和认识论（以《论确定性》为题出版）⁵。

这些作品大致是按《哲学研究》的思路前进的，不过，也有一些评论家因这些作品个性独特而造出"第三个维特根斯坦"一词来形容它们。⁶尤其在《论确定性》一书中，维特根斯坦处理了怀疑主义*这一问题。怀疑主义认为不可能存在对世界的真正知识，它自 17 世纪以来支配着许多哲学思想，但在《哲学研究》中这一问题基本未曾涉及。

> "四年前，我得以重读我的第一部著作（《逻辑哲学论》），并向人解释其中的思想。突然间，我想到应该将那些旧的思想与新的思想合在一起出版：只有与我旧的思想方式对比，并在其衬托下，我的新思想才能被正确地理解。"
>
> ——路德维希·维特根斯坦：《哲学研究》

整合

在整个职业生涯中，维特根斯坦专注于几个他感兴趣的大论题。他寻求对语言、思维与世界之间关系的理解。他渴望解释我们的词句是如何获得意义的，又是如何成功地**代表**世界上的事物的。

然而，维特根斯坦的后期与早期著作，不论在形式还是内容上，都形成了鲜明对比。这一对比如此鲜明，以至于评论家们有时称似乎有两个维特根斯坦。[7]《逻辑哲学论》一书写得极为精炼与严肃，结构也颇为复杂。而《哲学研究》一书的风格则更像谈话，它看起来没什么条理——由长长一组短小又有些松散的札记构成。一旦对它研究得更为深入，以上假设便会被证明是误导性的：该书有一个精心安排的结构。

维特根斯坦在两个时期的哲学立场也是截然不同的。实际上，《哲学研究》在某种程度上是在论证《逻辑哲学论》的相反立场。在序言中，维特根斯坦表示他的新著作"只有与我旧的思想方式对比，并在其衬托下才能被正确地理解。"[8]

在逻辑学的启发下，《逻辑哲学论》提出了一种抽象的语言观。它将语言的主要功能视为对世界的表象，并提出了"图像论"。根据这一理论，句子"描绘"现实，一个特定的句子的意义即它描绘世界的方式。相比之下，《哲学研究》则强调人类日常生活在决定我们使用的词句的意义上的重要性。它仅仅将表象视为语言的功能之一，反倒关注词句在具体语境中的使用。

意义

毫不奇怪，维特根斯坦最初的影响也是分为两轮的。《逻辑哲学论》在20世纪二三十年代产生了巨大影响，这在罗素和其他英国哲学家，如弗兰克·拉姆齐*的著作中都能反映出来。此外，这部著作对于逻辑实证主义哲学也极为重要。

因此，当维特根斯坦1929年重返哲学，开始重审并最终在《哲学研究》中完善其哲学观时，他在哲学界已是知名人物了。他的这部新作激起了哲学界读者的强烈兴趣，然而，因为他很少发表作品，所以他的思想最初基本上都是靠口耳相传的。

《哲学研究》成为与逻辑实证主义相去甚远的运动的一部分。它强调对语言使用的密切关注，影响了20世纪50年代的"日常语言哲学"。然而，这是一部难以简单归类的奇特作品。它也影响了心灵哲学、语言哲学、科学哲学等诸多领域的发展——尤其在维特根斯坦逝世后的几十年里。

大多数评论家都会同意，不论是好是坏，维特根斯坦的影响在最近几十年里已有些衰退了。[9] 尽管当今仍有些哲学家自称为"维特根斯坦派"，不过他们的人数已不比从前了。但不论如何，维特根斯坦的思想是现代哲学背景的重要组成部分，《哲学研究》也许是其影响最为持久的著作。

---

1. 路德维希·维特根斯坦：《逻辑哲学论》，D. F. 皮尔斯和B. F. 麦吉尼斯译，伦敦：劳特利奇出版社，1974年。
2. 这些手稿中最为重要的均已出版，有如下这些：路德维希·维特根斯坦：《哲学札记》，拉什·里斯编，雷蒙德·哈格里夫斯、罗杰·怀特译，牛津：布莱克威尔出版社，1975年；路德维希·维特根斯坦：《蓝皮书与棕皮书》，牛津：布莱克威尔出版社，1958年；路德维希·维特根斯坦：《哲学语法》，拉什·里斯编，安东尼·肯尼译，牛津：布莱克威尔出版社，1974年。
3. 值得注意的是，在该书的第4版中第2部分就被当成了独立的内容（彼得·哈克和乔基姆·舒尔特编，牛津：布莱克威尔出版社，2009年）。
4. 路德维希·维特根斯坦：《心理学哲学札记（第1卷）》，G. E. M. 安斯康姆译，牛津：布莱克威尔出版社，1980年；《心理学哲学札记（第2卷）》，C. G. 勒克哈特和M. A. E. 奥厄译，牛津：布莱克威尔出版社，1980年。

5. 路德维希·维特根斯坦:《论确定性》,丹尼斯·保罗和 G.E.M. 安斯康姆译,牛津:布莱克威尔出版社,1969 年。
6. 参见丹尼尔·莫亚夏洛克编:《第三个维特根斯坦》,奥尔德肖特:阿什盖特出版社,2004 年。
7. "两个维特根斯坦"这一观点的最有影响的支持者包括戴维·皮尔斯(《维特根斯坦》,伦敦:丰塔纳出版社,1971 年)与彼得·哈克(《见解与幻觉》,伦敦:克拉伦登出版社,1972 年)。
8. 路德维希·维特根斯坦:《哲学研究》,伊丽莎白·安斯康姆译,牛津:布莱克威尔出版社,2001 年,第 vii 页。
9. 最近一次讨论见彼得·哈克:《维特根斯坦:联系与争议》,牛津:牛津大学出版社,2013 年,第 xvii 页。

—————————————— 第三部分：学术影响

9 最初反响

要点

- 人们批评维特根斯抛弃了传统意义上的哲学工作。
- 《哲学研究》在维特根斯坦去世后才出版,而他身前几乎不对批评做出直接回应。
- 最初,维特根斯坦的思想并未见诸文章或著作,而是通过谈话和随意的笔记得以传播的。有一群崇拜者,通过这种非正式的形式听闻了他的观点,维特根斯坦思想早期便是这样被接受的。

批评

《哲学研究》直到 1953 年维特根斯坦逝世两年后才出版。在他身前,只有作为他学生的少数几位学者接触过这部著作,他们对他的这项工作深有共鸣。等到《哲学研究》全文出版后,评论家们才开始详细研究与评价维特根斯坦的观点,这时候真正意义上的批评与争论才出现。

有些思想较为传统的哲学家认为,维特根斯坦的后期著作主张抛弃传统的哲学任务:即增进我们对于世界的知识。曾钦佩并影响了维特根斯坦早期著作的罗素认为,其后期思想是在努力避免这门学科的艰难理论工作。[1] 维特根斯坦显然放弃了将哲学与科学相结合,罗素对于这点也深感不安。罗素始终认为哲学应与科学携手并进,哲学家与科学家也应该共事。这一观点看来是与维特根斯坦的新思想格格不入的。

同样,奥地利青年哲学家卡尔·波普尔*也认为,维特根斯坦的新思想使哲学变得浅薄。² 在波普尔看来，哲学跟科学一样，处理的都是关于世界本质的纯粹知性问题。而他认为维特根斯坦不再将哲学的工作视为解决问题，而仅仅视之为清除我们思考与言说世界时产生的谜团与无关紧要的混乱。波普尔认为，维特根斯坦的哲学已抛弃了对真实世界的探究，它探究的仅仅是语言。

> "早期的维特根斯坦沉溺于狂热而专注的思索，能深刻意识到困难的问题，这些问题我也同他一样觉得重要。他具有（至少在我看来）真正的哲学天赋。而后期的维特根斯坦则相反，他好像对严肃的思考疲乏了，并且发明了一种学说，把严肃思考这种活动搞得毫无必要。"
>
> —— 伯特兰·罗素：《我的哲学的发展》

回应

《哲学研究》是在维特根斯坦逝世以后出版的，因此他没有机会对成书以后的批评做出回应。即便在出版前，尽管他是活跃在剑桥大学的一名教师，也只是默默写作，不常谈论他工作的进展。跟大多数学者不同，他不会将未最终完成的成果拿到同行面前或会议上去展示。他也从来不在学术刊物上发表文章——只有《一些关于逻辑形式的札记》这篇文章是个例外。³

这样一来，维护与发展维特根斯坦思想的任务就落到了新一代哲学家的手里，他们曾深受维特根斯坦的影响。其中有不少曾是维特根斯坦在剑桥大学的学生，或与他在那里有私交。维特根斯坦指定其中几位——伊丽莎白·安斯康姆*、拉什·里斯*和冯·赖特*——为他的遗作管理人，负责《哲学研究》的出版准备工作。

诺曼·马尔科姆*和维特根斯坦的另一位学生彼得·吉奇*的著作也深受维特根斯坦的影响。

这些思想家提出了一个重要的观点，即维特根斯坦的方法与思想是能有效解决传统哲学关注的问题的。他们致力于解决的问题是维特根斯坦本人从未深究过的，并在其工作中表明了，维特根斯坦的影响其实能够被视为对哲学传统的丰富，而非破坏。

例如，伊丽莎白·安斯康姆写过一部关于行为与伦理*哲学的重要著作，明显可见维特根斯坦的影响。尤为值得注意的是她的《意图》[4]一书与《现代道德哲学》[5]一文。彼得·吉奇的《心灵行为》[6]一书赋予了心灵哲学以维特根斯坦的视角。诺曼·马尔科姆则致力于解决认识论*（关于知识的理论）的问题，其中也包含怀疑主义的问题。[7]

冲突与共识

自《哲学研究》出版后几十年来，赞同与反对维特根斯坦观点者围绕许多重要论题展开了激烈的争辩。其中一个论题为哲学的本质及其与科学的关系。哲学自然主义者*——他们认为科学与哲学应共同构成一项智力工作，且哲学问题能够并应当以科学方法来解决——反对维特根斯坦与他的支持者的观点。许多形而上学哲学家也相信，与维特根斯坦的看法相反，哲学的一部分职责正是建构解释世界的理论。

争论的第二个焦点是语言哲学。维特根斯坦派学者曾批判过这样的观点，即认为英语等语言中句子的意义是由句子为真的条件来判断的。他们相信，对于决定一句话的意义而言，重要的不是这句话的真值条件，而是这句话的使用。

争论的第三个焦点是心灵哲学。对于我们能否有意义地言说私人经验*这一问题,维特根斯坦派学者与他们的对手持不同意见。如果私人经验存在,那么便是一种仅仅属于特定某个人的感受或感觉,既不能用语言充分描述,也不能被他人知晓或理解。

哲学家们仍在争论着这些问题,而维特根斯坦的追随者们也在继续为这些争论贡献自己的见解。

---

1. 伯特兰·罗素:《我的哲学发展》,伦敦:艾伦与休恩出版社,1959 年,第 216—217 页。
2. 卡尔·波普尔:《猜想与反驳》,伦敦:劳特利奇出版社,2002 年,第 92—93 页。
3. 路德维希·维特根斯坦:"一些关于逻辑形式的札记",《亚里士多德学会会刊》1929 年第 9 卷(增刊):第 162—171 页。
4. 伊丽莎白·安斯康姆:《意图》,牛津:布莱克威尔出版社,1958 年。
5. 伊丽莎白·安斯康姆:"现代道德哲学",《哲学》1958 年第 33 卷:第 1—19 页。
6. 彼得·吉奇:《心灵行为:其内容与对象》,伦敦:劳特利奇出版社,1957 年。
7. 诺曼·马尔科姆:《做梦》,伦敦:劳特利奇出版社,1959 年。

10 后续争议

要点

- 《哲学研究》一书鼓励人们在语言哲学中应关注语言在实际与日常情境中的不同用法。
- 该著作促成了一群维特根斯坦派的思想家。他们将维特根斯坦的方法与思想运用于维特根斯坦本人未深入涉足的哲学领域,包括伦理学、宗教哲学以及认识论的多个分支。
- 当代思想家们依然在采用维特根斯坦的方法与思想来探索语言与心灵。

应用与问题

维特根斯坦令人耳目一新地提出对日常语言及语言在具体情境中使用的重视。在之前的语言哲学家,如弗雷格*等人的笔下,意义似乎是以语言自身的表达元素为基础的,是脱离其使用的情境的。

许多当代哲学家相信,构建一种语言的意义理论是可能的。这种理论可以告诉我们,在一种语言中与词句意义相关的**事实**是如何决定说话者的意谓的。一些著名人物,如唐纳德·戴维森*、迈克尔·达米特、戴维·卡普兰*等都支持这一观点。

简而言之,维特根斯坦对这一观点的质疑源于语境在理解话语中的极端重要性。仅仅凭借对一种语言的理解,并不足以让说话者理解现实中的话语。要充分理解所说的话,你必须也同时理解特定社会语境,以及说话者的目的与意图。

对建构语义理论感兴趣的哲学家不得不解释语境的重要性——

这是维特根斯坦反复强调的要点。对这一问题的响应可追溯至20世纪五六十年代英国语言哲学家保罗·格赖斯*的著作。他区分了语义学与语用学*，并将两者视为语言学中截然不同的两个部分。这一响应至今仍很流行。

语义学考察的是说话者通过理解一种语言能够理解什么。然而，这并非意味着理解人们在日常生活中的谈话。人们能用同样的词句在不同语境中表达不同的内容，尽管有可能产生歧义，但我们总能理解他们所要表达的。而语用学研究的则是能让我们理解对方意义的这种知识与技能。

例如，美国哲学家戴维·卡普兰[1]区分了"性质"与"内容"——意为一个句子的性质是固定的，而内容则因情境不同而有所改变。同样，语言学中的语境主义*者也曾试图构建理论来解释语境对于理解的绝对重要性。

> "我们提供的其实是关于人类自然史的评论；我们不提供什么奇闻逸事，而是一些无人怀疑的见解，它们之所以无人论及，是因为它们始终在我们眼前。"
>
> ——路德维希·维特根斯坦:《哲学研究》

思想流派

20世纪60年代以来涌现出了新一代的维特根斯坦派哲学家。这些思想家基本上跟维特根斯坦不曾有过深入的私交，但都从阅读他的作品，尤其是《哲学研究》中受到了启发。这群人中有许多都在美国，而不在英国，其中包括斯坦利·卡维尔*和科拉·戴蒙德*。

尚有许多传统哲学的领域维特根斯坦未在《哲学研究》中直接

涉及。维特根斯坦派哲学家的贡献之一，即将维特根斯坦的观点扩展到了他本人从未或甚少涉及的论题上。例如，《哲学研究》和维特根斯坦的其他著作实际上很少探讨伦理学，而戴蒙德等人则以维特根斯坦的视角出发研究伦理学，重视诸如"善良""正直"等伦理学概念在人们日常生活与交流中的使用方式。

《哲学研究》的早期读者或许也会认为传统的认识论，即关于知识的理论完全不可能出现在维特根斯坦的哲学语境中。他们也许会设想，语言与意义的问题可完全替代知识如何可能的问题。然而，汤普森·克拉克*与斯坦利·卡维尔等哲学家已揭示了认识论问题依然会产生。他们也论证了《哲学研究》中的思想是如何为认识论提供线索的。

特别的是，这些思想家还运用了维特根斯坦的思想来探讨怀疑主义这一古老问题。怀疑主义者认为，对世界的真实、客观的认识是不可能的。认识论者惯于应对这种对于知识的可能性的质疑，并已着手证明怀疑论者的谬误。克拉克、卡维尔等人探讨了怀疑主义的含义，以及在何种意义上它能被证实或证伪。[2]

当代研究

如今，如罗伯特·布兰登*、约翰·麦克道尔*等哲学家采用独特的维特根斯坦的方法来处理哲学问题——尽管他们在许多问题上意见并不一致。

维特根斯坦本人曾对建构庞大的哲学理论持批判态度，并力劝哲学家在工作中采用零敲碎打的方式。然而，并非他的每一个弟子都采纳了他的建议。例如，罗伯特·布兰登正致力于建构一种语义的方法论，有时被称为"推衍作用语义学"*。布兰登将维特根斯坦视为他这项工作的灵感之源。简言之，布兰登认为一个词句的意义是受其使用**方式**约束的，并将此与维特根斯坦"意义即使用"这一口号联系在一起。

维特根斯坦的其他追随者驳斥了这一太过理论化的方法，而宁愿继续追随维特根斯坦的步伐，致力于清除混乱，而非建构理论。采用该方法的最有影响的人物之一，即英国哲学家约翰·麦克道尔，尤为值得注意的是其1994年出版的《心灵与世界》这部著作。[3]

与其他维特根斯坦派学者一样，麦克道尔也认为我们不可能以一种他称之为"偏向一侧"的视角来看待语言与心灵。他声称，如果我们不采用正确的术语，便无法公正地处理心灵的问题。例如，只凭借神经科学*的术语，仅通过研究神经系统，尤其是人脑，我们是无法描述心理现象的。假如真的这样做了，那么我们将错失心灵的一些重要方面。如果不考察我们在日常生活中是如何描述与理解彼此的，那么我们就无法理解心灵。

---

1. 戴维·卡普兰："指示词"，《来自卡普兰的主题》，约瑟夫·阿尔莫格等编，牛津：牛津大学出版社，1989年。
2. 汤普森·克拉克："怀疑主义的遗产"，《哲学学报》1972年第64卷：第754—769页；斯坦利·卡维尔：《理性的诉求》，牛津：牛津大学出版社，1979年。
3. 约翰·麦克道尔：《心灵与世界》，马萨诸塞州剑桥：哈佛大学出版社，1994年。

11 当代印迹

要点 🔑

- 《哲学研究》依旧被学者或其他人广泛地研究,我们能够发现它在许多当代哲学家的著作中所产生的影响。不过,其影响似乎已不及 20 世纪五六十年代了。
- 该书挑战了表象主义——认为心灵状态可对世界之存在方式进行表象的观点。
- 哲学家们做出了回应,方式之一是将他们对传统哲学问题的看法与当代科学知识结合起来。

地位

哲学界对于《哲学研究》一书的价值与意义从未达成过共识。不过,要是说该书的影响力在今天已不及 20 世纪五六十年代了,倒或许属实。在索尔·克里普克与戴维·刘易斯等哲学家的影响下,形而上学已成为当代的焦点,它是与《哲学研究》的精神相违背的。形而上学专注于构造关于世界本质的理论,而非我们理解世界本质的方式。

总而言之,当今许多分析哲学家通过语言观察哲学与科学的联系时,已不像 20 世纪中叶的维特根斯坦及其同时代人那样,认为语言问题对于哲学来说至关重要。然而,这究竟是一时的潮流还是永久的事态,且让我们拭目以待吧。

该书的早期批评者关注的是其对心灵哲学的教益。尤其是维特根斯坦的"私人语言争论"似乎表明人们不能有意义地言说其私人感受,这便导致人们将他解释为某种行为主义*者——即认为一个句子的意义,如"保罗处于痛苦中"是凭保罗的外在行为,而非其内心感受才被理解的。

1982年，克里普克出版了《维特根斯坦论规则与私人语言》一书后[1]，关注点又很大程度上转回到了维特根斯坦的语言哲学观上。批评者反驳了克里普克对维特根斯坦的阐释，多数人也许会质疑其阐释的准确性，但他确实激发了一场新的争论，即如何将维特根斯坦的思想运用于当代对意义的探讨。

> "我们都站在，或者说，应当站在维特根斯坦的影子里，正如更早的那几代人曾站在康德的影子里……"
> ——迈克尔·达米特：《形而上学的逻辑基础》

互动

《哲学研究》挑战了心灵哲学的主导思想，该思想有时被称为表象主义，它也在很大程度上被理论心理学、认知科学*（对心灵的跨学科研究）所接受。表象主义认为心灵状态能对世界进行表象，它们具有真值条件：它们声称世界就是一种特定的方式。维特根斯坦在《哲学研究》中含蓄地质疑了这种理解心灵的方式。他提出，表象其实是一个很具体的概念，它有正规的用法，但不适用于所有的心灵状态。

更宽泛地说，维特根斯坦的著作对比了科学与哲学的实际工作。其中一个论题即提出科学家应以构造理论为己任，而哲学家则不应如此；哲学的作用乃澄清混乱，而非增加我们关于世界的理论知识。这便挑战了哲学家看待其学科的传统方式。

受维特根斯坦著作启发的批评家们对主流哲学提出了以上挑战。然而，这些批评家在多大程度上遵从了维特根斯坦的初衷，这是值得商榷的。对维特根斯坦哲学的正确阐释，至今仍然存在争议。

持续争论

　　心灵哲学中表象主义的拥护者修正了他们的观点，以便顾及维特根斯坦派学者的批评。表象主义者将心灵描述为对世界的表象或反映，或是对世界即一种特定方式的主张。近年来的许多争论都聚焦于感知的问题。在此问题上，表象主义者相信，看见桌上有个苹果即形成桌上有个苹果的心理图像（表象）。

　　在过去，这一观点往往是种假设，从未被正式提出并论证过。近来，该观点的拥护者开始构想一些论据来支持其主张了，有一部分原因是来自于维特根斯坦派学者们批评的压力。他们也更仔细地考察了究竟什么是感知表象这个问题。例如，哲学家苏珊娜·西格尔*便对这些问题进行了考察，旨在以提供更有力的辩护，反击对表象主义的批评。

　　尽管对维特根斯坦观点的回应并不一定来自单一的哲学视角，不过还是能够找到一条共同的主线。心灵哲学中的表象主义实质上是一场自然主义的运动，它巧妙地将心灵哲学跟认知科学和经验心理学的发展联系了起来。上述的语言哲学也采用了类似方法——试图以科学的方法来解答关于意义的问题。

　　总而言之，这些哲学家试图重新将哲学与科学融为一体，而这两门学科在维特根斯坦看来则是毫不相干的。他们所倡导的是一种维特根斯坦视为不可能，也不期许的更为科学的世界观。

---

1. 索尔·克里普克：《维特根斯坦论规则与私人语言》，牛津：布莱克威尔出版社，1982 年。

12 未来展望

要点 🗝

- 语言哲学和认识论（关于知识的哲学）中的语境主义者继续从维特根斯坦的思想中获取灵感。
- 《哲学研究》强调人在决定意义中的重要性。
- 《哲学研究》是一部复杂的著作，涉及了哲学的诸多领域。它将继续成为灵感与争议的源头。

潜力

维特根斯坦《哲学研究》一书在当今的影响力，也许已不及它出版后的头 20 年了。然而，它仍被十分广泛地阅读与研究。近来的两种流行的哲学观与维特根斯坦的观点有些亲缘关系，它们也许能影响该书在未来的影响力。这两种观点通常被称为"语境主义"：一种在语言哲学领域，另一种在认识论，即关于知识的理论的领域。

在语言哲学领域，语境主义认为一个人所说的话的意义是受其语境深刻影响的。当我用英语说了一句话，其意义不是由关于英语的事实决定的。要探明其意义，我们必须考察我说话的情境。可以说，这正是维特根斯坦在《哲学研究》一书中提出的观点。当代这一观点的支持者显然从维特根斯坦的思想中汲取了灵感。

在认识论领域，语境主义认为某个语境中的知识在另一个语境中也许就不成其为知识了。为应付日常需要，我可能相信我知道某一位同事是可靠的。但是我如果在法庭上当证人，那儿对证据有更高的要求，也许我就算不得知道这一事实了。维特根斯坦在其后期著作《论确定性》中提出过类似观点，但该观点也能在《哲学研究》中找到源头。

> "在维特根斯坦看来，哲学之所以陷入困境，并非因为它否认我们所知道的一切真实性，而是因为它想竭力逃脱人类的生活形式，可恰恰是生活形式赋予我们的表达以连贯性。他希望承认人类的局限性，这不至于使我们被自己的皮肤擦伤，也不至于因意识到自己无法逾越人类获取知识的条件而恼怒。"
>
> ——斯坦利·卡维尔：《维特根斯坦后期哲学的有效性》

未来方向

一些颇有影响的当代思想家，如美国哲学家查尔斯·特拉维斯，受维特根斯坦的启发而论证了语言哲学中语境主义的形式。特拉维斯提倡一种十分彻底的语境主义形式。在《意义的使用》[1]与《思想的基点》[2]这两本著作中，他援引《哲学研究》及维特根斯坦后期的其他著作来支持其论点，即认为语言使用的语境对于决定意义起到了深刻而广泛的作用。

另一位美国哲学家迈克尔·威廉姆斯*运用维特根斯坦的著作论证了认识论中的语境主义，特别在其《不自然的怀疑》[3]一书中。威廉斯声称维特根斯坦著作中的某些观念动摇了怀疑主义：该主义认为对世界不可能有真正的知识。怀疑论者曾争辩道，比如，我不能真正知道我的桌上有一只杯子，因为很可能我只是在做梦或产生了出现杯子的幻觉。

威廉姆斯认为，怀疑论者的质疑不必始终严肃对待。怀疑产生于特定的语境：例如，当我有具体理由认定事情不是它看起来那样的时候。在此，维特根斯坦又如一贯的那样教导我们，意义依赖于语境。怀疑或许在某个语境下是有意义的，而换个语境就未必了。

小结

维特根斯坦的《哲学研究》是 20 世纪分析哲学发展中的一部极为重要的著作。它对日常语言的前所未有的关注引发了语言哲学的革命。它揭示了这类语言的真正复杂性，也因此抛弃了哲学家从前所采用的语言的形式化模式。

该著作也使人们注意到了有关人类心灵之探讨的复杂与多样，从而给心灵哲学提供了新的动力，使该学科从此成为哲学研究的中心。它也对哲学的本质及其日常运作方式提出了一个关键问题：哲学究竟有什么用，应当用它来干什么？

《哲学研究》是一部内容十分丰富的著作。它仍会是哲学家和研究者的灵感源泉，其思想绝不会枯竭。尽管该书与众不同的形式使其难以理解（它由一长串彼此相关的札记，而非一整篇连贯的论证组成），但在启发哲学家创造出富有创见的作品方面，依然起着至关重要的作用。

若要总结该著作的意义，你也许会说，它标志着我们转向了对人的作用的重视。哲学中的一些关键概念，如真理、意义与表象，并非是脱离人类经验之抽象，维特根斯坦说道，若不考察其实际使用中的人类语境，就不能够理解它们。

维特根斯坦可被视为某种自然主义者，尽管如此，他也常常被视为反自然主义者。原因何在？因为他否认自然科学能最终解决包括哲学问题在内的所有知性问题。不过他也属于较广义上的自然主义者，他相信创造出哲学问题的思想超不出人类经验，反而还是人类经验的一部分，并在运用于生活中时才获得其意义。

  也许，《哲学研究》一书在未来的重要性，正在于它承认影响抽象的哲学问题的所有语词与概念都起源于人类。

---

1. 查尔斯·特拉维斯:《意义的使用：维特根斯坦的语言哲学》，牛津：克拉伦登出版社，1989 年。
2. 查尔斯·特拉维斯:《思想的基点》，牛津：牛津大学出版社，2006 年。
3. 迈克尔·威廉姆斯:《不自然的怀疑：认识论的实在论与怀疑主义的基础》，牛津：布莱克威尔出版社，1991 年。

术语表

1. **分析哲学**：20世纪具有影响力的一场哲学运动——尤其与英国、德国和美国相关——它重视逻辑、语言、以及哲学和科学的相互联系。

2. **人类学**：对人类与文化的科学研究。

3. **面相知觉**：指相同物体能以不同方式感知的一种现象。例如，一幅画既可以被感知为鸭子图，又可以被感知为兔子图。

4. **行为主义**：其观点为心灵状态应根据行为来理解——例如，愤怒本质上是表现为愤怒的一种行为。

5. **认知科学**：对心灵的跨学科研究，包含心理学、哲学、语言学与计算机科学等领域。

6. **概念分析**：一种通过对语词与概念进行分析以揭示其意义的哲学方法。

7. **语境主义**：其观点为词句的意义依赖于它们使用的情境。

8. **经验主义**：其观点为人类的所有知识皆来源于经验。

9. **认识论**：处理知识问题的哲学分支。

10. **伦理学**：处理道德与善的问题的哲学分支。

11. **信仰主义**：其观点为宗教信仰是以信念而非理性为基础的。

12. **格式塔学派**：20世纪早期主要由德国与奥地利心理学家组成的一个流派，主张知觉应从整体上来理解。沃尔夫冈·柯勒（1887—1967）也许能称得上其领军人物。

13. **推衍作用语义学**：其观点为词句的意义应根据与其他词句的推演作用，而非其真值条件来理解。

14. **意向性**：一种指向对象的或"关涉性"的状态。例如，恐惧具有意

向性，因为它总是**针对**某一事物的恐惧。

15. **语言游戏**：说话者为具体目的，并根据明确规则而使用词句的某个简单场景。

16. **逻辑学**：数学与哲学的一个分支，大致研究的是论证，尤其是推理。

17. **逻辑原子主义**：指一种哲学观点，主张一切有意义的句子都是由关于简单对象或逻辑原子的基本句或原子句按逻辑构造起来的。

18. **逻辑实证主义**：一场激进的哲学运动——兴盛于20世纪20年代后期，尤其在奥地利与德国——它强调对语言的逻辑分析。

19. **心灵实体**：存在于心灵中的事物，观念、思想、感觉、经验都可以算在内。

20. **形而上学**：研究实在的最终与根本组成部分，以及何为根本的存在的一个哲学分支。

21. **现代主义**：文学、音乐、艺术与建筑领域的一场运动，在20世纪早期尤为兴盛，其特征为对传统的决裂。

22. **自然主义**：在哲学领域，指哲学与科学从事的工作相同，运用的方法本质上也一致的观点。

23. **神经科学**：对神经系统，包括大脑在内的科学研究。

24. **日常语言哲学**：20世纪五六十年代的一个哲学流派，与牛津大学的联系尤为密切，该流派重视对语言使用的细致分析。

25. **作为治疗的哲学**：以消解知识上的疑问与混乱，而非获得关于世界的新的真理为宗旨的哲学著述。

26. **语用学**：对支配语言使用的规则与惯例的研究。

27. **私人经验**：不能用语言充分描述，因此只有具有该经验的人才能理解的一种经验。

28. **私人语言**：只能被一个人所理解的一种语言。

29. **表象主义**：其观点为语言与心灵的运作方式主要为准确或不准确地对世界进行表象。

30. **怀疑主义**：其观点为不可能获得关于世界的真正知识。

31. **唯科学主义**：其观点为最重要的知识问题都能以科学的方法解决。

32. **语义学**：对语言的意义的研究。

33. **感觉材料**：有些哲学家认为它们是感觉经验的直接对象的心灵实体。例如，视觉与听觉的直接对象有时被认为是色块与声音。

34. **社会学**：对社会的科学研究。

35. **神学**：对上帝的本质与属性的研究。

36. **第一次世界大战**（1914—1918）：卷入欧洲主要强国（尤其是德国、法国和英国）与包含美国、日本在内的世界其他强国的一场大规模冲突。

人名表

1. 伊丽莎白·安斯康姆（1919—2001），英国哲学家，维特根斯坦的学生之一。她或许算得上是战后维特根斯坦派哲学家的领军人物。

2. 约翰·郎肖·奥斯汀（1911—1960），英国哲学家，所谓的"日常语言"哲学学派的领军人物。他对语言哲学与知觉哲学均做出了重大贡献。

3. 阿兰·巴迪乌（1937年生），法国哲学家，撰写过形而上学与集合论方面的著作。

4. 路德维希·凡·贝多芬（1770—1827），德国作曲家，他的交响乐和室内乐常被认为是构建了古典主义和浪漫主义音乐时代的桥梁。

5. 戴维·布卢尔（1942年生），英国社会学家，其最广为人知的是创立了"爱丁堡学派"，该学派寻求在社会学范畴中理解科学。

6. 雅克·布弗莱斯（1940年生），法国哲学家，他捍卫与发展分析哲学的方式通常与英语世界联系更紧密。

7. 罗伯特·布兰登（1950年生），美国哲学家，其著作涉及语言哲学、心灵哲学、哲学史等广泛的领域。

8. 鲁道夫·卡尔纳普（1891—1970），德国哲学家，逻辑实证主义运动的领导者。他在逻辑学、语言哲学和科学哲学上均做出了贡献。

9. 斯坦利·卡维尔（1926年生），美国哲学家，其研究涉及维特根斯坦、哲学、艺术，尤其是电影等广泛的领域。

10. 汤普森·克拉克（1928—2012），美国哲学家，虽然仅发表过两篇短文，但在认识论领域颇具影响。

11. 尼古拉·哥白尼（1473—1543），波兰天文学家与数学家，主张日心说，根据这一学说，位于太阳系中心的是太阳而非地球。

12. 唐纳德·戴维森（1917—2003），美国语言哲学家，其语言哲学与心灵哲学领域的著述自 20 世纪 70 年代以来产生了巨大的影响。

13. 科拉·戴蒙德（1937 年生），美国哲学家，其研究涉及伦理学、语言哲学、维特根斯坦等广泛的领域。

14. 迈克尔·达米特（1925—2011），英国哲学家，他既是一位颇具影响的语言哲学家，又是弗雷格著作的重要阐释者。

15. 戈特洛布·弗雷格（1848—1925），德国数学家、哲学家，尽管其逻辑学与语言哲学著作在身前鲜为人知，但之后却在这两个领域引发了革命。

16. 西格蒙德·弗洛伊德（1856—1939），德国心理学家，也是精神分析的创始人。他提出无意识的驱动与抑制系统决定了人类的大部分行为。

17. 彼得·吉奇（1916—2013），英国哲学家，其著作涉及逻辑学、语言、哲学史等广泛的领域。

18. 赫伯特·保罗·格赖斯（1913—1988），英国语言哲学家，他在哲学和语言学领域均被认为是一位重要人物，也是语用学这门学科的创始人。

19. 彼得·哈克（1939 年生），英国哲学家，他是维特根斯坦作品最为重要的阐释者之一。

20. 马丁·海德格尔（1889—1976），德国哲学家，与现象学派存在联系，该学派 20 世纪早期兴盛于德国和法国，旨在从主体第一人称的视角研究意识。

21. 德里克·贾曼（1942—1994），英格兰电影制片人，他以实验性电影风格和对争议性主题的处理而闻名。

22. 伊曼努尔·康德（1724—1804），德国哲学家，著有《纯粹理性批判》（1781），他或许称得上是近代最具影响力的一位哲学家。

23. 戴维·卡普兰（1933 年生），美国哲学家，曾在语言哲学领域贡献了重要的思想。

24. 古斯塔夫·克林姆特（1862—1918），澳大利亚画家，他的作品以风格的标新立异与直白的性爱著称。

25. 索尔·克里普克（1940年生），美国哲学家，他在逻辑学、语言哲学及其他众多领域均做出了贡献，被公认为当代最重要的哲学家之一。

26. 托马斯·库恩（1922—1996），美国哲学家与科学史家，他对历史条件在科学知识形成中的重要性的强调最广为人知。

27. 约翰·麦克道尔，英国哲学家，其作品涵盖了众多主题，包括亚里士多德、伦理学、认识论及心灵哲学。

28. 诺曼·马尔科姆（1911—1990），美国哲学家，他在认识论领域具有贡献，也是美国第一代研究维特根斯坦的学者之一。

29. 沃尔夫冈·阿玛多伊斯·莫扎特（1756—1791），奥地利作曲家，他的交响乐、弥撒曲、歌剧以及协奏曲被认为是古典音乐时代极为重要的作品。

30. 卡伊·尼尔森（1926年生），加拿大哲学家，在宗教哲学领域著述颇丰。

31. 戴维·泽弗奈亚·菲利普（1934—2006），威尔士哲学家，深受维特根斯坦的影响，其著述内容广泛，涉及伦理学、文学及宗教。

32. 卡尔·波普尔（1902—1994），奥地利哲学家，是20世纪最著名的科学哲学家之一。

33. 弗兰克·拉姆齐（1903—1930），英格兰哲学家，同时也是经济学家与数学家。他是维特根斯坦著作的第一批评论家之一，并参与了《逻辑哲学论》第一个英译本的翻译工作。

34. 拉什·里斯（1905—1989），英国哲学家，他将维特根斯坦的思想运用到了宗教哲学领域。

35. 艾弗·阿姆斯特朗·理查兹（1893—1979），英格兰文学批评家，他是一位诗人，同时也撰写了一批颇具影响的文学理论著作。

36. 理查德·罗蒂（1931—2007），美国哲学家，当代哲学思潮的激烈批判者，其著述涉及文学、语言哲学等广泛的领域。

37. 伯特兰·罗素（1872—1970），英国哲学家、逻辑学家、社会评论家，及政治活动家。其早期在逻辑学与数学基础领域的工作对分析哲学起到了奠基作用。

38. 吉尔伯特·赖尔（1900—1976），英国哲学界的领军人物，经常将他与所谓的"日常语言"学派联系在一起。他对心灵哲学的贡献最大。

39. 阿诺尔德·勋伯格（1874—1951），奥地利作曲家，其音乐极具变革性，尤其是打破了传统的和声。

40. 弗朗茨·舒伯特（1797—1828），奥地利作曲家，他的许多交响乐、室内乐和歌曲被认为是早期浪漫主义音乐的杰出代表。

41. 约翰·塞尔（1932年生），美国哲学家，他对语言哲学与心灵哲学均做出了贡献。

42. 苏珊娜·西格尔，美国哲学家，现任哈佛大学埃德加·皮尔斯哲学教授，主要致力于认识论与心灵哲学的研究。

43. 查尔斯·特拉维斯（1943年生），美国哲学家，他是语言哲学中激进语境主义的著名拥护者。

44. 戴维·福斯特·华莱士（1962—2008），美国作家，在小说与非小说作品的创作上均具有知名度。

45. 阿尔弗雷德·诺斯·怀特海（1861—1947），英国数学家与哲学家，以数理逻辑上的基础性工作与形而上学方面的研究而闻名。

46. 迈克尔·威廉姆斯（1947年生），美国哲学家，曾撰写了大量有关认识论与维特根斯坦的著作。

47. 乔治·亨里克·冯·赖特（1916—2003），芬兰哲学家，其著作涉及逻辑学和语言哲学等广泛的领域。

WAYS IN TO THE TEXT

KEY POINTS

- Ludwig Wittgenstein (1889–1951) was an Austrian philosopher who became one of the most important thinkers of the twentieth century.

- Published in 1953, *Philosophical Investigations* discusses language, the human mind, and the nature of philosophy itself.

- *Philosophical Investigations* is *the* major statement of Wittgenstein's later philosophical work and one of the most important and influential books ever written on the philosophy of language and the philosophy of mind.

Who Was Ludwig Wittgenstein?

Ludwig Wittgenstein was born in Vienna, Austria in 1889. As a young man he studied engineering, but his mathematical work in this area led him to developing an interest in the philosophy of mathematics and then philosophy in general. Wittgenstein read and admired the philosopher Bertrand Russell's* book, *The Principles of Mathematics*. In 1911, he went to England to study with Russell at the University of Cambridge, but left to fight for Austria in World War I.* During the war he wrote a philosophical book, the *Tractatus Logico-Philosophicus*,[1] which became very influential. The work focused on showing how language and the world relate to each other, explaining how our words and sentences acquire meaning. Believing he had now solved philosophy's main problems, Wittgenstein gave up philosophy and became a schoolteacher in Austria.

In 1929, Wittgenstein returned to Cambridge to teach and

began a new phase in his philosophical thinking. There he argued against many of the things he once believed, including what he had written in the *Tractatus*. He now thought that the *Tractatus* account of language was too far removed from our everyday experience of using language.

Wittgenstein did not, however, publish his new ideas during his lifetime. Instead he discussed them with friends and students. He wrote many sets of notes and drafts for a book setting out his ideas, though he was never quite happy with what he had written. His students compiled and edited the material included in *Philosophical Investigations*, publishing the book after his death in 1951.

Investigations, like the *Tractatus*, gave rise to new schools of thought in philosophy. Wittgenstein is now widely regarded as one of the greatest thinkers of the twentieth century, and many people see *Philosophical Investigations* as his best work.

What Does *Philosophical Investigations* Say?

Published in 1953, Ludwig Wittgenstein's *Philosophical Investigations* is a complex work. In it, Wittgenstein does not focus on a single argument, but instead develops a number of themes, the most important of which is about language. He believes that philosophical problems arise from the confused use of language and that the way to solve those problems is by clarifying language use—not by discovering new facts or inventing new theories.

Investigations provides an alternative to conventional ways of thinking about philosophy. Philosophers often view themselves as producing general theories about the world. Wittgenstein argues that this is a mistake. He also challenges the popular belief at the time that he wrote *Investigations* that science can solve all important intellectual problems. To him, philosophical problems are quite different from scientific ones and cannot be solved by finding out more about the world.

If we want to understand both language and mind, Wittgenstein thinks we must study ordinary uses of language. We must look at how people use language in their everyday lives. This will differ greatly in different societies and cultures. So when Wittgenstein asks: what is the meaning of a word or sentence? He answers: the meaning lies in the way it is used in language. In other words, to understand meaning, we should look at how different people, cultures, and communities use words and sentences because meaning is essentially a public and social phenomenon.

Wittgenstein criticizes the idea that the German mathematician and philosopher Gottlob Frege,* among others, proposed: that meanings are abstract. Wittgenstein contended instead that the needs of everyday life determine the way we use words and sentences. We use language to make jokes, buy food, or play games, he says. Abstract rules do not govern the way we use language, and the way people have used language in the past does not tell us how to use words now.

Wittgenstein argues, too, that private language*—language that can only one person can understand—is impossible. So language cannot take its meaning from a particular individual's inner thoughts because meanings are not private mental states.

Language depends on public use to have meaning.

Investigations moves away from the abstract and highlights the importance of human context. Wittgenstein argues that the problems of philosophy cannot be understood independently of the human situations in which they arise. In order to understand abstract philosophical ideas like truth and meaning, we need to look at how human beings actually live their lives.

The book is still very widely studied and discussed. It is certainly one of the most influential philosophical works of the twentieth century. However, few people would say that it has been entirely understood. Interpreters still argue about what it means, while philosophers and other readers continue to find new insights and ideas in it.

Why Does *Philosophical Investigations* Matter?

Philosophical Investigations is a difficult work to understand, partly because it deals with difficult and complex questions. But Wittgenstein also writes in an unusual way. Rather than putting forward the themes of the book in a straightforward argument, he offers remarks on and illustrates those themes. As a result, even though individual sections are often easy to read, it becomes hard to see how they all fit together.

Nevertheless, *Investigations* can still be pleasurable to read. Wittgenstein writes well, so the book can be enjoyed on a literary level. It is full of interesting ideas, metaphors, and suggestions. His idea of comparing the ways that we use language to the playing of games, for example, has had an impact on many readers. They have found that the book inspires them to think in new ways. Wittgenstein himself says in the preface that his aim is to stimulate readers to develop thoughts of their own.

The book is relevant to many different disciplines. It is certainly a revolutionary work of philosophy, but it has also had an impact on a number of other areas. Its emphasis on how social environment shapes language was important to linguists. In addition, Wittgenstein's thoughts on how we use language to do things other than to state truths has influenced both theologians* and literary critics. For example, theologians are interested in how religious language not only states supposed facts about God, but also expresses emotions.

Philosophical Investigations has also had an effect outside academia, inspiring writers, poets, and film-makers, including I. A. Richards,* Derek Jarman,* and David Foster Wallace.* That is because Wittgenstein emphasizes the importance of everyday life and language and the differences between societies and cultures. This still matters today when we are much more aware of the importance of cultural differences than writers had been before Wittgenstein's time.

The book also offers a method from which readers can learn. Wittgenstein approaches difficult problems by finding new ways to look at them. He believes that the best way to solve a problem is to formulate it correctly. Often, once we know what questions to ask, then it becomes easier to find the solution. Suppose, for example, that we ask for the meaning of the word "please." We would go wrong if we looked for a single meaning that the word stands for.

Instead we should look to how it is used. We say "please" in order to acquire something, to be polite, and so on.

Wittgenstein thinks philosophical problems come about because of the way we use language. So if we clarify the words and sentences that we use, we will come to see the world much more clearly. Wittgenstein believes that philosophical problems are essentially linguistic confusions. It is a controversial view. To what extent are philosophical problems really a language issue? But, whatever the case, Wittgenstein's method of approaching problems by examining the ways in which we describe them is useful.

---

1. Ludwig Wittgenstein, *Tractatus Logico-Philosophicus*, trans. D. F. Pears and B. F. McGuinness (London: Routledge, 1974).

SECTION 1
INFLUENCES

MODULE 1
THE AUTHOR AND THE HISTORICAL CONTEXT

KEY POINTS

- *Philosophical Investigations* is one of the most important works of philosophy written in the twentieth century. It has influenced the way we think about language, the mind, and philosophy itself.
- Wittgenstein knew some of the most important contemporary thinkers in Britain and Germany. While he took account of their work, he was also a fiercely independent thinker who subjected others' views and his own to intense scrutiny.
- Wittgenstein wrote two great works of philosophy: the *Tractatus Logico-Philosophicus* and *Philosophical Investigations*. *Investigations* makes profound criticisms of the thinking in the *Tractatus*.

Why Read This Text?

Published in 1953, *Philosophical Investigations* is one of the most important philosophical works of the twentieth century and the final, authoritative statement of Ludwig Wittgenstein's thought. In his youth, Wittgenstein had put forward bold and original philosophical ideas in his book, the *Tractatus Logico-Philosophicus*. However, when he was older, he changed his opinions radically, and he suggests in *Investigations* a very different approach to philosophy.

Wittgenstein introduces in the book a range of central philosophical issues concerning language, the human mind, and the nature of philosophy itself. His views on each of these topics have been discussed ever since. In each case, he proposes that we pay close attention to the actual situations in which human beings find themselves, and he emphasizes careful attention to detail rather than the formulation of grand theories. Instead of inventing a theory to show how some words become the names of objects, he says, we should look at how names are *actually used* in everyday speech.

Wittgenstein's approach to the philosophy of language and mind has been influential. But so has his attitude to philosophy itself. Wittgenstein sees philosophical problems as a result of confused or ill-understood uses of language and believes the way to solve these problems is to clarify how language is used.

> *"The figure of Ludwig Wittgenstein exerts a very special fascination that is not wholly explained by the enormous influence he has had on the development of philosophy this century. Even those quite unconcerned with analytical philosophy find him compelling. Poems have been written about him, paintings inspired by him, his work has been set to music."*
>
> ——Ray Monk, *Ludwig Wittgenstein: the Duty of Genius*

Author's Life

Ludwig Wittgenstein was born in Austria in 1889 into a family of extremely wealthy Viennese industrialists. It was a highly cultured and, in particular, musical family. His brother, Paul Wittgenstein, was a successful concert pianist, and several other members of the family were musically talented. Wittgenstein himself was musically gifted, although his tastes were conservative. He had a passion for the classical German and Austrian tradition of Mozart,* Beethoven,* and Schubert* and a disdain for the music of his own day.[1]

Following his father's wishes, Wittgenstein studied engineering at the University of Manchester in England and while there he became interested in logic and the philosophy of mathematics. In 1911, he left Manchester without taking his degree to study at the University of Cambridge with Bertrand Russell,* the eminent philosopher and logician (someone who studies logic*). Russell had written an important book about the foundations of mathematics, *The Principles of Mathematics*,[2] which Wittgenstein had read and admired.

Wittgenstein left Cambridge at the outbreak of World War I* and joined the Austrian army. While a soldier, he wrote his early masterpiece, the *Tractatus Logico-Philosophicus*. First published in 1921, the *Tractatus* gives a general theory of language, showing how words and sentences acquire their meaning. Wittgenstein believed that philosophical questions arose from problems about meaning and language, and the *Tractatus* showed how to solve such problems. In that work, he thought he had solved the main problems of philosophy, so he gave up philosophy and became a schoolteacher in Austria.

In the meantime, the *Tractatus* became enormously influential both in England and in Europe. By the time Wittgenstein returned to Cambridge in 1929, he had gained a great reputation as an original thinker prepared to challenge accepted beliefs. However, he had changed his own views radically since writing the *Tractacus*. While nobody knows for sure, that may have been the reason he returned to philosophy and Cambridge—he believed that he had work left to do. At Cambridge, his lectures and philosophical discussions on logic and the philosophy of language, mind, and mathematics attracted many students, eager to understand and develop his ideas. During his life, Wittgenstein's thoughts spread by word of mouth and the informal circulation of lecture notes and manuscripts. These notes and manuscripts were to form the basis of the *Investigations*.

Wittgenstein worked as a teacher and scholar at the University of Cambridge from 1929 until his death in 1951 at the age of 62. He developed most of the ideas behind the *Investigations* there and also wrote parts of the book during extended stays in isolated parts of Norway and Ireland.[3] He produced most of the text in its current form between about 1936 and 1949.

Author's Background

When Wittgenstein was young, Vienna was a place of great cultural creativity. The psychoanalytical theories of Sigmund Freud* (treating emotional and mental problems by having a patient talk about dreams, feelings, and memories),* the music of Arnold Schoenberg,* and the art of Gustav Klimt* all emerged in that city in the early twentieth century. Although Wittgenstein disliked modernist* music that broke with previous traditions, he was nevertheless influenced by the innovative cultural environment in Vienna and maintained a strong interest in Freud's theories. His one architectural work, a house on the Kundmanngasse in Vienna that he designed for his sister, shows modernist influences.

In the preface to *Philosophical Investigations*, Wittgenstein writes of the "darkness of this time."[4] Since he was writing in January 1945, many readers have assumed that he was referring to World War II*. However, biographer Ray Monk has argued that Wittgenstein was actually referring to the cultural environment of the time—in particular, the dominance of the natural sciences.[5] Although Wittgenstein was familiar with and interested in science, by the time he wrote *Investigations*, he had come to think that its intellectual importance was dangerously exaggerated. His later work can be seen as an early reaction against what is today sometimes called "scientism": * the view that science is the only important way of understanding the world.

---

1. Ray Monk, *Ludwig Wittgenstein: the Duty of Genius* (London: Vintage, 1991), 13.
2. Bertrand Russell, *The Principles of Mathematics* (London: Allen and Unwin, 1903).
3. Monk, Ludwig Wittgenstein, 361ff and 520ff.
4. Ludwig Wittgenstein, *Philosophical Investigations*, trans. Elizabeth Anscombe (Oxford: Blackwell, 2001).
5. Monk, *Ludwig Wittgenstein*, 486.

MODULE 2
ACADEMIC CONTEXT

KEY POINTS

- Many modern philosophers, especially since Immanuel Kant,* were concerned with understanding the scope and nature of human thought.
- In the early twentieth century, philosophers such as Gottlob Frege* and Bertrand Russell* came to believe that the best way to study human thought was to study language.
- Wittgenstein agreed with Frege and Russell on the importance of language, but he emphasized the many different uses to which it can be put.

The Work in Its Context

In the late eighteenth century, the great German philosopher Immanuel Kant introduced a new approach to philosophy that remained influential into the twentieth century and beyond. Kant looked at philosophical problems by asking how the structure of the human mind and human thought affect our knowledge of the world. He believed that studying the ways in which we think about the world can throw light on the traditional philosophical questions about truth, meaning, and knowledge.

Kant called this approach the "Copernican turn." The great mathematician and astronomer, Copernicus,* had revolutionized Renaissance* thought in the early sixteenth century by reversing the usual view of the solar system. Instead of the established view that the sun revolved around the earth, he said that the earth revolved around the sun. Similarly, Kant believed, we could explain human knowledge by assuming it was shaped by the structure of the human mind, rather than just the structure of the world around us.

Kant's project was to understand the limits of human knowledge and reason, because then we could know why some of the central philosophical questions had never been answered. Such questions included whether God exists and whether the universe is eternal. They cannot be answered, Kant thought, because they attempt the impossible: to respond to questions beyond the limits of human reason.

> "Only with Frege was the proper object of philosophy finally established: namely, first, that the goal of philosophy is the analysis of the structure of thought; secondly, that the study of thought is to be sharply distinguished from the study of the psychological processes of thinking; and, finally, that the only proper method for analysing thought consists in the analysis of language."
>
> —— Michael Dummett, *Truth and Other Enigmas*

Overview of the Field

In the twentieth century, philosophers put Kant's question in a linguistic form. They saw a direct link between the limits of thought and the limits of language, of what can be expressed in words. They therefore came to see language as central to philosophy.

When Wittgenstein wrote *Investigations*, the development of what is often called "analytical philosophy,"* had revolutionized philosophy in the English-speaking world. That strand of philosophy focused on logic,* careful attention to language, and a respect for science.

A central figure in this development was the German philosopher and mathematician Gottlob Frege, who published his *Foundations of Arithmetic* in 1884.[1] Frege made an enormous contribution to the philosophy of language. He aimed to analyze thought by examining the language in which thought is expressed. But, unlike Wittgenstein, his analysis was geared towards scientific and mathematical uses of language.

Another key figure was Wittgenstein's mentor, Bertrand Russell, the British philosopher and logician.* Russell saw language's main purpose as giving an accurate representation of the world. He thought that if language could be made more accurate and precise, the representation of the world would be better too. He used the tools of modern logic* to achieve this aim. Russell expressed these views in influential works including the article "On Denoting,"[2] and his great multi-volume work of mathematical logic, co-authored with Alfred North Whitehead,* *Principia Mathematica*.[3]

Academic Influences

It is difficult to know specifically which philosophers had an impact on Wittgenstein, as he generally does not cite authors or give conventional references. But he does mention Gottlob Frege as a crucially important influence. One way to understand

Investigations is as a modification of Frege's own philosophy, extending the focus on language to non-scientific uses.

During Wittgenstein's early years at the University of Cambridge (1911–14), Russell was his teacher. And Wittgenstein also came to have an acknowledged influence on Russell. However, by 1936, when Wittgenstein began to write *Investigations*, the two philosophers were no longer close friends and had little personal contact. Wittgenstein disliked the popular, non-technical works that Russell was writing by that time. Russell, in turn, disliked Wittgenstein's later work, but he was still an important influence on his student. The difference between the two men was that Russell thought the aim of language was the representation of reality—forming a sort of picture of the world—whereas Wittgenstein stressed the many different purposes for which language can be used. And where Russell thought that language had to be refined and made more precise, Wittgenstein insisted that ordinary language is adequate as it is.

In many respects, *Investigations* runs directly counter to the most important movement in the philosophical scene of the 1930s, one that Frege, Russell, and the early Wittgenstein himself greatly influenced: logical positivism.* A group of Austrian and German philosophers known as the "Vienna Circle," the most important of whom was Rudolph Carnap,* had developed the movement, which emphasized the logical analysis of language. They were empiricists,* people who believe all human knowledge comes from experience. Their view was that only sentences that could be empirically verified—confirmed by experiment or observation—

had meaning.

So, for example, it would be meaning*ful* to ask what time it is in Japan, because that can be checked. But it is meaning*less* to ask whether God is good, or whether Mozart or Beethoven is the better composer, because (the logical positivists thought) such things cannot be confirmed or denied. On that basis, they criticized much of traditional philosophical, ethical, religious, and artistic conversation as meaningless.

Wittgenstein disagreed. He thought that the scientific use of language is only one use among others, so in fact there could be no general way of deciding what was meaningful, as the logical positivists thought.

---

1. Gottlob Frege, *Foundatons of Arithmetic*, trans. J. L. Austin (Oxford: Blackwell, 1950).
2. Bertrand Russell, "On Denoting," *Mind* 14 (1905): 479–93.
3. Bertrand Russell and A. N. Whitehead, *Principia Mathematica* (Cambridge: Cambridge University Press, 1910–13).

MODULE 3
THE PROBLEM

KEY POINTS

- Philosophers were interested in the question: how do words and sentences get their meaning?
- Gottlob Frege* had understood meaning in terms of truth: the meaning of a sentence, he thought, is given by the conditions under which it is true. The logical positivists* thought that the meaning of a sentence is given by the way we decide whether it is true or false.
- Wittgenstein rejected the idea that there is a single way of analyzing language. He said we should look at the ways language is used to understand its nature.

Core Question

Ludwig Wittgenstein never gives us a clear statement of his intentions in writing *Philosophical Investigations*, so it is difficult to identify the core question that it is designed to answer. One useful way of approaching the book, however, is to think of it as addressing the question: how do our words and sentences get their meanings? That question was crucial, too, to the philosophers who had come just before Wittgenstein.

However, the book also addresses a broader question: how do our mental states—our beliefs, desires, expectations, memories, and so on—get their meanings? In this second question, the word "meaning" must have a different (though related) sense. This question concerns what philosophers call the "intentionality"* of these mental states, or how they are directed at things. How, for example, does a desire come to be a desire *for* a particular thing? How does my desire for ice cream come to be a desire specifically for ice cream?

These are perhaps the most-fundamental questions that can be asked about language and the mind. They have come to be particularly urgent in modern times because of the success of natural science. For instance, scientists can explain more and more of the world in terms, for instance, of animal behavior. Human behavior, however, is less easily explained scientifically, precisely because so much of it involves meanings and intentions. So, the nature of meaning becomes a pressing intellectual question.

> "The aims of this school are less spectacular than those of most philosophers in the past, but some of its achievements are as solid as those of the men of science."
> —— Bertrand Russell, *History of Western Philosophy*

The Participants

Wittgenstein's most important philosophical influence, Gottlob Frege, had concentrated on formulating a semantic* theory—that is, a theory of the meaning of language. He argued that the "unit of meaning" is the thought, and that the meaning of a thought lies in its "truth condition," or the way the world has to be for the thought to be true.

Bertrand Russell* took up Frege's ideas in *The Philosophy of Logical Atomism*, a book[1] based on lectures that he delivered in 1918. In that work, Russell explains how our talk and thought about the world acquires meaning. According to him, we are able to think about the world because our mental states represent states of affairs in the world (representationalism).* This representational relation between mental states and real states of affairs is the starting point: it explains the various types of thought we can have about the world. So, if I say, "The cat is on the chair," I am giving a representation of the world. If the cat *is* on the chair, what I say is true. If it isn't, what I say is false. Either way, I have represented the cat as being on the chair.

Wittgenstein also agreed with this viewpoint in the *Tractacus Logico-Philosophicus*, but he later came to believe that this is only one way to use language among many others. So, if I say, "I'm tired," I may merely be telling you how I'm feeling. But I may also be trying to get you to make the tea so I can put my feet up. In that case, the real reason that I say, "I'm tired," is not in order to represent the world at all, but to influence your actions.

Russell believed that we could discover how our thoughts hook on to the world by analyzing them into their constituent parts (logical atomism).* If we do this, we discover that these constituent parts are private perceptions and experiences—what Russell called "sense data."* Ultimately, it is only sense data that we can name as constituent parts, as it is only with sense data that we ever have direct perceptual contact.

When Wittgenstein was developing the ideas of *Philosophical Investigations* in the 1930s and 1940s, the most vigorous philosophical movement of the era, logical positivism*, was increasingly dominating the philosophical debate. Like Frege and Russell, the logical positivists focused on linguistic meaning. They believed that the role of philosophy was to discover the correct analysis of sentences and thereby discover their true meaning. Indeed, that was the only way to assess whether they were meaningful at all.

The logical positivists put forward a theory that only sentences that can be empirically* verified—confirmed by experiment or observation—count as meaningful. So, for example, abstract, religious, or metaphysical* (what there fundamentally *is*) discussion is literally meaningless. Take a sentence like, "There is a daisy growing on top of Kilimanjaro." You can check whether that is true or not by looking for a daisy growing on top of Kilimanjaro. But it is not possible to check whether a sentence like, "God loves us," is true. Therefore, according to the logical positivists, it has no meaning whatsoever.

The Contemporary Debate

In *Investigations*, Wittgenstein rejects many of the ideas of Frege, Russell and the logical positivists. He rarely cites other philosophers by name, though Frege and Russell (his former teacher) are among the few exceptions. In key passages of the *Investigations*, Wittgenstein is clearly responding to Russell, even where he does not mention him by name.[2]

Wittgenstein says we should focus on the uses of language rather than on words and sentences that are divorced from their contexts. He encourages us to examine "language games:" particular, concrete situations where people use language for specific purposes. Those encompass the scientific uses of language that Frege and the logical positivists concentrated on. More controversially, Wittgenstein also includes literary and religious uses of language, which the positivists had condemned as meaningless.

Wittgenstein rejects the idea that there is a general rule for understanding meaning and such a thing as a single correct analysis of a sentence. He believes that we can analyze thoughts in different ways, depending on their purpose.

For example, we might explain the sentence, "John is a bachelor," by saying, "John is not married." But the second sentence is neither more basic nor more fundamental than the first. It is simply more useful for the purpose of explaining the sentence to someone who does not understand the word "bachelor." The logical positivist idea that philosophy acts as an aid to scientific work by clarifying the real meaning of sentences cannot be maintained.

Or think again of the sentence, "I'm tired." It might be a dispassionate report of how I'm feeling, or it might be an attempt to get you to make the tea. Two utterly different things, but the sentence is the same. The important point is: I'm using the same sentence for different purposes on two different occasions. Since meaning, for late Wittgenstein, is use, it's not sentences that have meaning, but the particular circumstances in which they are said. Suppose I say, "God loves us." I might be reporting on the way I take God to be, or trying to cheer you up, or making a joke. These are all utterly different uses of the same sentence. You can't ask whether the sentence is meaningful or not. So, according to

Wittgenstein, it follows that logical positivism is false.

Wittgenstein dismisses Russell's ideas wholesale, particularly the abstract notion of "representation." Instead, he says, we should look to our specific aims and purposes in concrete situations if we want to understand our thoughts and talk about the world. The meaning of language comes from a shared, public environment, not from personal experience. Wittgenstein therefore rejects Russell's concept of "sense data," too.

Although Wittgenstein denounced the ideas of his predecessors, he understood profoundly their arguments. He had absorbed the genuine lessons of modern logic* and modern philosophy and, as a result, *Philosophical Investigations* was regarded as a powerful attack on his fellow philosophers.

---

1. Bertrand Russell, *The Philosophy of Logical Atomism* (London: Routledge, 2009).
2. For example, § (Remark) 79 clearly alludes to Russell's theory of descriptions, and the discussions of private language and inner experience beginning around § (Remark) 243 engage with Russell's views on perception.

MODULE 4
THE AUTHOR'S CONTRIBUTION

KEY POINTS

- Wittgenstein summarized his view in the slogan "meaning is use."
- Wittgenstein's view placed a new emphasis on the analysis of ordinary uses of language and the role that language plays in everyday life.
- In the work of his predecessors, and even in Wittgenstein's own earlier work, *scientific* uses of language were often emphasized as particularly important. In *Philosophical Investigations*, Wittgenstein sees science as just one use of language among many others.

Author's Aims

Ludwig Wittgenstein once described his aim as getting people "to change their style of thinking."[1] His purpose in *Philosophical Investigations* is not so much to convince people of specific philosophical guiding principles as to uncover the roots of common mistakes and confusions. In particular, Wittgenstein wants to lead us away from broad, general theories about language and the mind and encourage us instead to pay attention to particulars.[2] In philosophy, unlike physics and biology, there is no need to form these general theories, Wittgenstein says, because the subject is difficult to understand. Rather, our ordinary ways of thinking and talking about the world are fine as they are. Philosophical problems arise only when we misuse the tools we already have at our disposal. Taking it to an extreme, if Wittgenstein's aims were successful, the problems would disappear and the philosophers would just have to keep quiet.

Some commentators[3] believe that Wittgenstein thought the aims of philosophy should be to prevent bad thinking, not to arrive at truths. They say he practiced philosophy as a kind of therapy*, aiming simply to remove intellectual problems and confusions. *Philosophical Investigations* does, however, contain many insights into the traditional problems of the philosophy of language, the philosophy of mind, and the philosophy of mathematics. Its approach is certainly against coming up with theories, but it also makes a contribution to positive philosophical thought.

Wittgenstein's aims influenced the way he wrote. His tone is conversational and it does not have the structure of a conventional written argument. Voices appear, representing the sort of philosophical approaches that Wittgenstein wants to challenge, and then he responds in his own voice. This unusual structure makes it difficult to interpret Wittgenstein's intentions. As a result, contemporary debate on the book focuses not only on the arguments, but also on how best to understand what Wittgenstein hoped to achieve with it.

> *"For a large class of cases—though not for all—in which we employ the word 'meaning' it can be defined thus: the meaning of a word is its use in the language."*
> —— Ludwig Wittgenstein, *Philosophical Investigations*

Approach

Wittgenstein's approach to language emphasizes the specific uses that speakers give to words and sentences. In order to understand how language works, he invented the idea of a "language game."* A language game is a simple situation in which language is used for a particular purpose. The moves in the game are the words of the speakers. As in a game of chess, definite rules govern those moves.

For example, at the beginning of *Investigations*, Wittgenstein describes a language game played by people building a house. A builder calls out words like "slab," "pillar," and so on, and an assistant fetches the appropriate item. Wittgenstein's thought is that if we ask what words like "slab" *mean* for builders, we must describe what they *do* with these words.

Wittgenstein believed a speaker of a language like English plays many different language games and that the use of a given word will depend on the particular situation. There are no definite rules governing the use of the language as a whole, only within specific situations. So, to understand what speakers of the language are doing on a particular occasion, we need to understand which language game they are playing.

One result of this approach is that, for Wittgenstein, the scientist is merely playing one language game among many. Scientific usage has no special status in understanding language use as a whole, and Wittgenstein placed far less emphasis on scientific usage than his predecessors.

Contribution in Context

Although Wittgenstein criticized the views of fellow philosophers Gottlob Frege* and Bertrand Russell,* he also learned a great deal from them. One way of looking at his work is that he deepened and extended their insights. They concentrated on the use of scientific language, and Wittgenstein broadened the debate to cover other things that we do with language.

One can find some parallels with Wittgenstein's criticisms of this earlier school of philosophical thought in other writings of the period. There are some similarities, for example, with the "ordinary language philosophers,"* who were based largely at the University of Oxford. One was J. L. Austin,* who also believed that philosophy should clear up linguistic confusions and that language is best understood by examining how ordinary speakers use words. The philosopher Gilbert Ryle,* like Austin and Wittgenstein, made a careful examination of language use. He also shared with Wittgenstein an emphasis on the importance of behavior. If we want to understand the nature of mental states such as anger, we should look at the ways in which angry people behave.

But while Ryle was sympathetic to Wittgenstein's ideas, Austin at first couldn't understand them. Perhaps that was because of the unconventional way in which they were presented: not as a traditional academic argument, but as a series of remarks, illustrations, and examples. In general, Wittgenstein's critical response to logical positivism,* with its logic-based analysis of language, and mainstream analytical philosophy* was more radical and challenging than that of other critics, including Austin and Ryle. That meant it took much longer for Wittgenstein's work to be accepted into the academic mainstream.

---

1. Ludwig Wittgenstein, *Lectures and Conversations on Aesthetics* (Oxford: Blackwell, 1967) § (Remark) 28.
2. Ludwig Wittgenstein, *Philosophical Investigations*, trans. Elizabeth Anscombe (Oxford: Blackwell, 2001) § (Remark) 109.
3. See in particular the essays in Rupert Read and Alice Crary, eds., *The New Wittgenstein* (London: Routledge, 2000).

SECTION 2
IDEAS

MODULE 5
MAIN IDEAS

KEY POINTS

- According to *Philosophical Investigations*, the meaning of a word lies in how it is used in language. So, in order to understand the meanings of words and sentences, we need to look at the specific situations in which they are used.
- The understanding of language depends on objects and behavior that are observable by at least some people. The meanings of words cannot depend on purely private sensations.
- The ideas are not presented as a single flowing argument. Instead Wittgenstein makes a large number of interrelated remarks, showing the many connections between the themes he discusses.

Key Themes

Wittgenstein's *Philosophical Investigations* contains several main themes. The first is the idea that *meaning* is best understood in terms of *use*. The second is about his discussion of rules and how they are followed. The third concerns argument against "private language"*—a language understood by only one person.

The book begins with Wittgenstein's views about language and meaning,[1] where he puts forward his idea that the meaning of an expression comes from its use in human life. "For a *large* class of cases—though not for all—in which we employ the word 'meaning,'" he writes, "it can be defined thus: the meaning of a word is its use in the language."[2] In particular, he attacks the idea that names of things and people get their meaning simply by being attached to individual things.

Wittgenstein then discusses following rules.[3] Here he argues that following a particular rule (for example, a rule about the correct use of a word i. e. that "bachelor" applies only to unmarried adult males) is not just about interpreting a particular word correctly. Instead, he says that following rules is about reaching agreement with others on how we are to speak and act.

Next comes the "private language argument."[4] Wittgenstein argues that words for mental states such as "pain" do not get their meaning from being associated with the personal—meaning private—experiences of the speaker. These are experiences that only the speaker knows. Instead, like other terms, words like "pain" get their meaning from communication with others and from public use.

> "The best that I could write would never be more than philosophical remarks; my thoughts were soon crippled if I tried to force them on in any single direction against their natural inclination. And this was, of course, connected with the very nature of the investigation. For this compels us to travel over a wide field of thought criss-cross in every direction. The philosophical remarks in this book are, as it were, a number of sketches of landscapes which were made in the course of these long and involved journeyings."
> —— Ludwig Wittgenstein, *Philosophical Investigations*

Exploring the Ideas

Wittgenstein points to language's broad range of uses. He argues that we can only understand speech and behavior by referring to people's specific aims and the particular circumstances of their lives. Language use is part of what Wittgenstein calls a "form of life."[5]

Languages like English and French do not merely function to communicate thoughts. They also express the attitudes and ways of life of English and French speakers. Take expressions like, "Thank God," or "for the greater glory of God." Someone who uses these expressions is expressing a certain attitude to life. If a listener does not understand these expressions, we cannot explain them merely by telling them who God is. It may be that their culture is so different that they cannot understand the *attitude* that is being expressed.

Wittgenstein says that if the lion could speak, we would not understand him.[6] Why not? It is not that we and the lion would not talk about the same things. Most likely, we would both have words for antelopes and mountains. But that wouldn't be enough for understanding to take place, because the lion's way of life and outlook on the world would be significantly different. In short, we have different forms of life.

Wittgenstein believed we need to look at the particular circumstances in which language is used. He calls these "language games,"* in which words and sentences are used according to certain rules and for particular purposes.

He argues that we can only understand the difference between correct and incorrect uses of words and sentences by looking at language games. This does, however, lead to the question: what governs the correctness or incorrectness of future uses of language?

Wittgenstein argues that nothing in the past use of any word or expression is strong enough to determine how it will be used in the future. There are always different ways of interpreting past use to fit with new uses.

In general, no rules concerning the use of words are sufficiently strong that they can determine what counts as "correct" use in new circumstances. Rules can always be re-interpreted, so different future behaviors can be described in a way that makes them fit with any existing rule. Wittgenstein writes, "No course of action could be determined by a rule, because every course of action can be made out to accord with the rule."[7] When situations change, very often we need to make new decisions about how to use language.

Wittgenstein applies the same conclusion to private mental entities*—ideas, thoughts, feelings—as he does to abstract rules: that they do not govern language use. Mental representations can be thought of as rules that are spelled out in the mind rather than on paper, and like such rules, they can be re-interpreted to fit with different sorts of future applications.

More generally, Wittgenstein argues against the idea that any language could take its meaning from the private mental life of the individual. We are tempted to think that the language we use to describe feelings and sensations is personal. For example, the word "pain" as *I* use it gets its meaning from *my* private sensation of pain. But Wittgenstein argues that no word could work like this. The correctness and incorrectness of words must have public standards against which they are measured and cannot depend on private experience.* If they did, there would be no way of checking whether they were being used correctly or incorrectly.

Language and Expression

Philosophical Investigations is a beautifully written work that has a great deal of literary merit. Its language is not overly formal, is understandable and is largely free of technical terminology. As a result, it can be a very enjoyable book to read.

However, that does not mean it is easy to understand. This is partly because Wittgenstein doesn't state his ideas and arguments clearly. Instead, he allows them to grow out of a wide-ranging discussion that covers many areas. In his preface, he writes that the nature of his investigation means that the reader must "travel over a wide field of thought criss-cross in every direction."[8]

The result is that the book is difficult to place in conventional academic philosophy. Different readers can interpret it differently, and it can be very hard to see just how Wittgenstein's ideas line up with those of other philosophers.

There are two distinct views on Wittgenstein's writing style. Some commentators—for example, Michael Dummett, the British philosopher,*—suggest that the book's style is the result of Wittgenstein's personality, rather than its philosophical content. They reason that Wittgenstein's views could have been expressed in a more conventional philosophical form, backed up by clear and explicit arguments.[9] Others, such as American philosopher Stanley Cavell,* argue that the style of *Investigations* is essential to its message.[10] Part of Wittgenstein's point, Cavell says, is that the attempt to formulate general theories leads to mistakes and confusion, and that we can only come to a clear view of language by careful consideration of specific cases.

---

1. Ludwig Wittgenstein, *Philosophical Investigations*, trans. Elizabeth Anscombe (Oxford: Blackwell, 2001), §§ (Remarks) 1–184.
2. Wittgenstein, *Philosophical Investigations*, § (Remark) 43.
3. Wittgenstein, *Philosophical Investigations*, §§ (Remarks) 185–242.
4. Wittgenstein, *Philosophical Investigations*, §§ (Remarks) 243–363.
5. Wittgenstein, *Philosophical Investigations*, §§ (Remarks) 19, 241.
6. Wittgenstein, *Philosophical Investigations*, §§ (Remarks) 223.
7. Wittgenstein, *Philosophical Investigations*, §§ (Remarks) 201.
8. Wittgenstein, *Philosophical Investigations*, vii.
9. See, for example, Michael Dummett, "Wittgenstein's Philosophy of Mathematics," in *Truth and Other Enigmas* (London: Duckworth, 1978).
10. Stanley Cavell, *The Claim of Reason* (Oxford: Oxford University Press, 1979, xx.

MODULE 6
SECONDARY IDEAS

KEY POINTS

- Wittgenstein believes that philosophy should not attempt to gain new knowledge. Instead, it should solve misconceptions that arise from confusions in our thought.
- "Aspect perception"* means experiences in which we can hear or see things in different ways. Wittgenstein uses such experiences to discuss the relationship between perception and thought.
- Wittgenstein's views have been widely studied, but philosophers have not yet accepted all of his ideas.

Other Ideas

Philosophical Investigations is a broad-ranging book that touches on many topics. It contains several subsidiary themes: Ludwig Wittgenstein's understanding of philosophy; his critique of conceptual analysis* (the analysis of words and concepts to discover their meaning), and the notion of what is called "aspect perception"* (how the same object can be seen in different ways). This can also be thought of as "seeing as."

In the book, Wittgenstein says, "Philosophical problems arise when language goes on holiday."[1] His idea is that philosophical confusions occur when we use language in unsuitable ways. It is not that there is anything wrong with a particular word or phrase when it is used in its original, natural way. It goes wrong when it is applied outside its normal context. He imagines someone asking,

"What time is it on the sun?"[2] This question has no definitive answer, but not because there is anything vague or unclear about asking for the time in normal circumstances.

The method of conceptual analysis had been important to Wittgenstein's immediate philosophical predecessors, such as Bertrand Russell* and the logical positivists.* Conceptual analysis involved studying language by looking at words and sentences to analyze their real meaning. Wittgenstein argues that this method is flawed: there is no such thing as a single correct analysis of a given sentence.

The second part of the book focuses on the philosophy of psychology,* although Wittgenstein did not review this part for publication. Some commentators, including the British philosopher Peter Hacker,* argue that it should not be considered part of *Investigations* at all. The best-known passages look at aspect perception—a type of experience that the Gestalt school* of psychologists studied, in which, for example, one sees two different figures in the same shape—as it pertains to the relationship between perception and thought.

Wittgenstein uses the example of a diagram that can be seen either as a picture of a duck or a picture of a rabbit. If you look at the diagram for a long time, it seems to switch repeatedly between being a duck-picture and a rabbit-picture. Such "aspect switches" are interesting because they can be interpreted either as seeing something new or as having a new thought, so that thought and perception seem to overlap. "Hence the flashing of an aspect on us," Wittgenstein writes, "seems half visual experience, half thought."[3]

> "What is your aim in philosophy? To shew [show] the fly the way out of the fly-bottle."
>
> —— Ludwig Wittgenstein, *Philosophical Investigations*

Exploring the Ideas

Wittgenstein presents his negative critique of conceptual analysis clearly and without room for doubt. This is one of the points in the book in which a reader can identify an explicit argument. However, his attack on the conception of analysis is very specific to Russell, who saw the analysis of concepts as the main point of philosophy. This makes understanding Wittgenstein's point difficult for readers who are not familiar with Russell's writings.

Wittgenstein gives his views of this method, but he also presents an alternative by introducing language games:* imagined scenarios in which people use language for specific purposes that differ from, but also throw light on, our own. The focus changes from words and sentences to specific utterances and uses of language.

Picture two people in different countries where it's raining. Both make the comment "It's raining." It's the same sentence but it is also two different utterances that could have been said for different reasons. One person might have been telling someone to take an umbrella; the other might have been making idle conversation. Wittgenstein's point is that the specific context creates the meaning.

Wittgenstein does not give the language-game method an

explicit definition. Instead he gives many examples of language games. He urges us, "Don't think, but look!"[4] Here Wittgenstein's literary abilities are put to good use and he describes his scenarios vividly. He presents, for example, a community where the language consists of the use of words like "slab" and "pillar," and he imagines how different the life is in that community.[5] He displays a striking imaginative skill in conceiving it, so many readers who are not familiar with philosophical methods have nevertheless intuitively grasped the language-game method in *Investigations*.

In his discussions on aspect perception, Wittgenstein returns again and again to the problem of whether an aspect experience is a matter of seeing or of thinking. It seems to have features of both. On the one hand, it looks as though the interpretation of the duck/rabbit as a duck is akin to having a thought. On the other hand, the fact that it is a visual interpretation means it is more like *seeing* a new object, or seeing the same object in a new way.

While opinions differ on how these examples relate to the other themes of *Investigations*, Wittgenstein does draw one explicit parallel: just as with pictures for a person viewing them, the way in which words and sentences are understood depends on the background and point of view of the person who hears them. A speaker of English, for example, has a different response depending on whether the word "bank" is used to refer to a financial institution or to the bank of a river.

Overlooked

Vast amounts have now been published about Wittgenstein's

Philosophical Investigations. It is unlikely that many sections of the text, or aspects of its argument, have been entirely overlooked. Still, it is possible to identify certain features that have been relatively neglected and may yet prove to be of lasting philosophical significance.

Although Wittgenstein's philosophy of language has been studied extensively, certain elements have still not been entirely explored. One interesting question is what lessons Wittgenstein's approach for contemporary philosophy of language and linguistic theory might hold. Most important is the role of context in understanding. Speakers of a language rely on contextual factors, as well as knowledge of the language, to understand each other. Crucially important to our mutual understanding is the fact that we live distinctly human lives: "If a lion could talk," Wittgenstein writes, "we could not understand him."[6]

Scholars may have overlooked this point in the past because some influential interpretations of Wittgenstein's views on language make them seem out-dated. In particular, the American philosopher John Searle* considered Wittgenstein to be a descriptivist when it came to proper names—in other words, that Wittgenstein believed that the meaning of a name could be identified by a cluster of descriptions.[7] For example, the meaning of the name "Moses" might be identified with such descriptions as "the man who led the Israelites out of Egypt." This view has become unpopular in recent philosophy, particularly since the publication of *Naming and Necessity*[8] by Saul Kripke,* an American philosopher and logician. However, it is quite possible to argue that Wittgenstein was *not* a descriptivist in this sense, simply because he was against all general theories.

---

1. Ludwig Wittgenstein, *Philosophical Investigations*, trans. Elizabeth Anscombe (Oxford: Blackwell, 2001), § (Remark) 38.
2. Wittgenstein, *Philosophical Investigations,* § (Remark) 350.
3. Wittgenstein, *Philosophical Investigations*, 168.
4. Wittgenstein, *Philosophical Investigations*, § (Remark) 66.
5. Wittgenstein, *Philosophical Investigations*, § (Remark) 6.
6. Wittgenstein, *Philosophical Investigations*, 190.
7. John Searle, "Proper names," *Mind* 67 (1958) 166–73.
8. Saul Kripke, *Naming and Necessity* (Oxford: Blackwell, 1980).

MODULE 7
ACHIEVEMENT

KEY POINTS
- Wittgenstein inspired a new way of thinking about philosophy and the relationship between philosophy and science.
- In recent decades, there has been a return to metaphysics*—what makes up reality—and theorizing about the nature of the world in philosophy. As a result, Wittgenstein's influence has declined.
- Wittgenstein's ideas have been influential in many disciplines other than philosophy.

Assessing the Argument

Ludwig Wittgenstein inspired new ways of thinking both about philosophy itself and the relationship between philosophy and science. His conception of philosophy continues to be influential today. According to Wittgenstein, philosophy is not about formulating general theories about the world. Instead, its aim should be to clear up conceptual confusions.

His views on the difference between science and philosophy have also been influential. He believes that the two have quite different purposes. The aim of science is to gain new knowledge of the world and explain it by formulating theories. Philosophy, by contrast, contributes not knowledge but understanding. Through philosophical discussion, we come to a better understanding of our own thoughts and ideas.

Some commentators, perhaps most prominently the American

philosopher Richard Rorty,* have argued that Wittgenstein has shown that philosophy has come to an end.[1] It is no longer an intellectual discipline, insofar as its aim was to increase our knowledge of the world, and science can now perform this function. And although philosophy has aspired to discuss deeper questions concerning goodness or the meaning of life, it has been superseded by imaginative literature. This school of thought is based on a controversial reading of Wittgenstein's arguments *against* explanatory theories in philosophy.

> "A picture held us captive. And we could not get outside it, for it lay in our language and language seemed to repeat it to us inexorably."
> —— Ludwig Wittgenstein, *Philosophical Investigations*

Achievement in Context

Within the philosophical community no consensus has formed about the value and significance of *Philosophical Investigations*. Some philosophers[2] believe the book has radical lessons for philosophy that have still not been fully accepted or understood. They cite, in particular, Wittgenstein's argument that the careful investigation of language shows that traditional philosophical investigations into the metaphysical* nature of the world (the fundamental elements of reality) are based on confusions. Others[3] view the work as dogmatic and unconvincing. They continue to pursue traditional philosophical questions that Wittgenstein believed to be senseless or misleading.

It is probably true that *Investigations* is today less influential than it was in the 1950s and 1960s. Metaphysics—the branch of philosophy that deals with the fundamental things that make up reality— is once again popular under the influence of philosophers such as Saul Kripke* and David Lewis,* and that philosophical approach goes against the spirit of *Investigations*. Wittgenstein's view of philosophy—one concerned with our ways of conceiving of the world—has been replaced by theorizing about the nature of the world itself. Many analytical philosophers* do not take questions of language to be as central to philosophy as their predecessors in the middle of the twentieth century. It remains to be seen, however, whether this is a temporary trend or a permanent state of affairs.

Wittgenstein's early influence was mostly restricted to Britain and North America. Several of his students became academics in British and American universities and introduced serious discussion of his work there.[4] However, even on the European Continent, let alone the rest of the world, Wittgenstein's work was associated with the narrow field of English-speaking analytical philosophy. This has changed in recent years, with the work of philosophers such as Jacques Bouveresse* and Alain Badiou* in France, along with a new interest in exploring connections between the work of Wittgenstein and his German contemporary Martin Heidegger.*[5]

Limitations

Wittgenstein's work has had an impact across the humanities and social sciences, not just in philosophy. One field in which his influence has been particularly notable is theology.* As a result of the concepts in *Philosophical Investigations*, some theologians have moved away from thinking of religion as a metaphysical doctrine (a set of ideas that are taught or are believed to be true) or a theory about the origin or nature of the world.[6] Their focus has changed from religious doctrine to religious practice—what actually happens in a religion. More accurately, Wittgensteinian theologians insist that religious doctrines should be interpreted within the context of religious practice. Fundamentally, this is an argument about how religious language should be understood, and they apply Wittgenstein's notion that meaning is use: if we wish to understand the meaning of religious terms, we must look at how they are used.

Some authors, most prominently the Canadian philosopher Kai Nielsen,* characterized the Wittgensteinian view of religion as "fideism."* Fideism is the view that religious belief is or should be based on faith rather than reason. However, Wittgensteinian religious thinkers, such as D. Z. Phillips,* have disputed that characterization as a misinterpretation.[7] Wittgenstein does not hold that religious beliefs cannot be criticized on philosophical or scientific grounds.

Sociology* and anthropology* are other areas where Wittgenstein has had an influence—in particular, his emphasis that the world view of the subject is what is important, with its aim of describing a situation from the subject's point of view and in terms of his or her own practices.

A notable example is the subfield of sociology of science. A prominent recent trend in this area is to look at different scientific viewpoints from their own point of view. According to this approach, shifts from one scientific viewpoint to another are not explained as progressive moves towards what the theorist knows to be the truth. Instead, we should understand the work of past scientists in *their* own terms, using the concepts that they themselves used. An early enthusiast for this approach was Thomas Kuhn,* whose *Structure of Scientific Revolutions*[8] explicitly acknowledges Wittgenstein's influence. A more recent example is the work of David Bloor,* author of *Wittgenstein, Rules and Institutions*.[9]

Wittgenstein has had an influence in a range of other disciplines, including literary criticism, art history, and education.[10] These applications stray quite far from the topics that Wittgenstein explicitly discusses in *Philosophical Investigations*—so much so that it is impossible to say whether he would have approved of them.

---

1. Richard Rorty, *Philosophy and the Mirror of Nature* (Princeton, NJ: Princeton University Press, 1979).
2. For recent examples, see Paul Horwich, *Wittgenstein's Metaphilosophy* (Oxford: Oxford University Press, 2013) and Charles Travis, *Thought's Footing* (Oxford: Oxford University Press, 2006).
3. See, for example, Timothy Williamson, *The Philosophy of Philosophy* (Oxford: Blackwell, 2007).
4. Important examples are Norman Malcolm at Cornell, Elizabeth Anscombe at Oxford and Peter Geach at Birmingham and Leeds.
5. See for example Lee Braver, *Groundless Grounds: a Study of Wittgenstein and Heidegger* (Cambridge, Mass.: MIT Press, 2012).
6. See for example Fergus Kerr, *Theology after Wittgenstein* (Oxford: Blackwell, 1986).
7. Kai Nielsen and D. Z. Phillips, *Wittgensteinian Fideism?* (London: SCM Press, 2005).
8. Thomas Kuhn, *The Structure of Scientific Revolutions* (Chicago: University of Chicago Press, 1962).
9. David Bloor, *Wittgenstein, Rules and Institutions* (London: Routledge, 1997).
10. See, for example, James Guetti, *Wittgenstein and the Grammar of Literary Experience* (Athens GA: University of Georgia Press, 1993).

MODULE 8
PLACE IN THE AUTHOR'S WORK

KEY POINTS

* Wittgenstein was concerned throughout his career with the relationship between language and thought.
* *Philosophical Investigations* was the major statement of his later philosophy, and it contrasts with his early work, the *Tractatus Logico-Philosophicus*.
* *Tractatus* and *Philosophical Investigations* are Wittgenstein's most famous and widely studied works, but the latter has probably exerted the greatest influence on subsequent thinkers.

Positioning

Ludwig Wittgenstein's philosophical career divides naturally into two main periods. From 1911 to 1914 he worked on philosophy at the University of Cambridge. *Tractatus Logico-Philosophicus*,[1] the short book he wrote while fighting in World War I* and as a prisoner of war in Monte Cassino in Italy at the end of the war, expressed his early philosophical views. He then gave up philosophy and worked as a schoolteacher in rural Austria, before returning in 1929 to Cambridge to study philosophy again and begin a new period that lasted until his death.

Philosophical Investigations is the central work of Wittgenstein's mature period. It is the culmination of his research between 1929 and 1949. Other manuscripts and sets of remarks from the 1930s have been published, and they show how

Wittgenstein's thought developed, culminating in the ideas that appear in *Investigations*.[2]

Wittgenstein's students edited and published *Philosophical Investigations* after his death. Although he prepared most of the manuscript in its current form, it is impossible to say whether he would have made further changes before publication. Scholars also disagree about whether the section generally known as "Part Two" of *Investigations* should be regarded as part of the book or as a separate work.[3]

Wittgenstein continued to write on philosophical matters in the few years between the completion of the *Investigations* and his death in 1951. Although he did not produce any more book-length works, several of his typescripts from this period have since been published, organized according to subject matter. Two major themes were the philosophy of psychology (writings on this topic were published under the title *Remarks on the Philosophy of Psychology*)[4] and the theory of knowledge (*On Certainty*).[5]

These works broadly continue the direction of *Investigations*, though they are sufficiently distinctive that some commentators have coined the term "third Wittgenstein" to describe them.[6] In *On Certainty* in particular, Wittgenstein deals with the problem of skepticism,* the view that genuine knowledge of the world is impossible. This problem had dominated much of philosophical thought since the seventeenth century, but it is largely absent from *Investigations*.

> "Four years ago I had occasion to re-read my first book (the Tractatus Logico-Philosophicus) and to explain its ideas to someone. It suddenly seemed to me that I should publish those old thoughts and the new ones together: that the latter could be seen in the right light only by contrast with and against the background of my old ways of thinking."
>
> ——Ludwig Wittgenstein, *Philosophical Investigations*

Integration

Throughout his career, Wittgenstein was interested in certain broad topics. He sought to understand the relationship between language, thought, and the world. He wanted to explain how our words and sentences get their meaning and how they succeed in being *about* things in the world.

Nevertheless, Wittgenstein's later writings contrast sharply with his earlier ones, both in style and content. The contrast is such that commentators sometimes speak as if there were two Wittgensteins.[7] The *Tractatus* is written in a highly compressed and somber way and has a complex structure. The style of *Investigations* is far more conversational, and it can appear quite formless—it consists of a long series of short and somewhat loosely related remarks. On closer investigation, this assumption turns out to be misleading: the book has a carefully planned structure.

The philosophical positions of the two periods are also very different. In fact, in some ways, *Investigations* argues the opposite of the *Tractatus*'s position. In his preface, Wittgenstein suggests that his new work can "be seen in the right light only by contrast with and against the background of my old way of thinking."[8]

The *Tractatus* presented an abstract conception of language inspired by logic.* It saw the main function of language as the representation of the world, and it put forward a "picture theory." According to that theory, sentences "pictured" reality, and the meaning of a given sentence was how it pictured the world. In contrast, *Investigations* emphasizes the importance of ordinary human life in determining the meanings of the words and sentences that we use. It sees representation as only one function of language among many, and it concentrates instead on the use of words and sentences in specific situations.

Significance

Unsurprisingly, Wittgenstein's initial influence also came in two waves. The *Tractatus* was enormously influential in the 1920s and 1930s, as can be seen in the works of Bertrand Russell* and other English philosophers such as Frank Ramsey.* Moreover, it was extremely important in the philosophy of logical positivism.*

So Wittgenstein was already famous within the philosophical community when he returned to philosophy in 1929 and began the reconsideration of his philosophical position that was to culminate in *Investigations*. His new work aroused great curiosity among readers of philosophy, but since he published very little, at first his ideas spread mostly by word of mouth.

Investigations became part of a movement away from logical positivism. It influenced the "ordinary language philosophy"* of the 1950s, with its emphasis on careful attention to language use. But it is too quirky a work to fit neatly into any one category. It also influenced developments in the philosophy of mind and language, the philosophy of science, and many other areas—particularly in the first few decades after Wittgenstein's death.

Most commentators would agree that, for better or worse, Wittgenstein's impact has waned somewhat in recent decades.[9] Although some philosophers today would call themselves "Wittgensteinians," they are fewer in number than in the past. Nevertheless, his ideas are an important part of the background of modern philosophy, and *Philosophical Investigations* is probably his most enduringly influential work.

---

1. Ludwig Wittgenstein *Tractatus Logico-Philosophicus*, trans. D. F. Pears and B. F. McGuinness (London: Routledge and Kegan Paul, 1974).
2. The most important of these manuscripts have been published as Ludwig Wittgenstein, *Philosophical Remarks*, ed. Rush Rhees, trans. Raymond Hargreaves and Roger White (Oxford: Blackwell, 1975); Ludwig Wittgenstein, *The Blue and Brown Books* (Oxford: Blackwell, 1958) and Ludwig Wittgenstein *Philosophical Grammar*, ed. Rush Rhees, trans. Anthony Kenny (Oxford: Blackwell, 1974).
3. Notably, it is treated as such in the fourth edition of the book, edited by Peter Hacker and Joachim Schulte (Oxford: Blackwell, 2009).
4. Ludwig Wittgenstein, *Remarks on the Philosophy of Psychology*, trans. G. E. M. Anscombe, vol. 1 (Oxford: Blackwell, 1980) and *Remarks on the Philosophy of Psychology*, trans. C. G. Luckhardt and M. A. E. Aue, vol. 2 (Oxford: Blackwell, 1980).
5. Ludwig Wittgenstein, *On Certainty*, trans. Denis Paul and G. E. M. Anscombe (Oxford: Blackwell, 1969).
6. See Daniele Moyal-Sharrock ed., *The Third Wittgenstein* (Aldershot: Ashgate, 2004).

7. Influential proponents of the "two Wittgensteins" view include David Pears, *Wittgenstein* (London: Fontana, 1971), and Peter Hacker, *Insight and Illusion* (Oxford: Clarendon Press, 1972).
8. Ludwig Wittgenstein, *Philosophical Investigations*, trans. Elizabeth Anscombe (Oxford: Blackwell, 2001), vii.
9. For a recent discussion, see Peter Hacker, *Wittgenstein: Connections and Controversies* (Oxford: Oxford University Press, 2013), xvii.

SECTION 3
IMPACT

MODULE 9
THE FIRST RESPONSES

KEY POINTS
- People criticized Wittgenstein for abandoning the work of philosophy as it was traditionally understood.
- *Philosophical Investigations* was published after Wittgenstein's death, and while he was still alive, he rarely responded directly to criticisms.
- At first, Wittgenstein's ideas were not published in articles or books, but circulated through conversations and informal notes. A group of admirers who heard about his views in this informal way shaped the early reception of his ideas.

Criticism

Philosophical Investigations was not published until 1953, two years after Ludwig Wittgenstein's death. During his lifetime, only a small number of scholars who were his own students had access to the text. They were deeply sympathetic to his project, and it was only after *Investigations* was published in full that substantive criticism and debate began as critics started to study and evaluate Wittgenstein's arguments in detail.

Some more traditionally minded philosophers thought Wittgenstein's later work proposed abandoning the traditionally accepted task of philosophy: to contribute to the advancement of our knowledge of the world. Bertrand Russell,* who admired and influenced Wittgenstein's early work, thought his later ideas were an attempt to avoid the hard theoretical work of the discipline.[1] He was also disturbed by Wittgenstein's apparent move away from the uniting of philosophy with science. Russell had always thought that philosophy ought to be in partnership with science, with philosophers and scientists engaged in a common activity. That idea seemed incompatible with Wittgenstein's new thinking.

Similarly, the young Austrian philosopher Karl Popper[*] believed that Wittgenstein's new ideas trivialized philosophy.[2] According to Popper, philosophy deals with genuine intellectual problems about the nature of the world, just as science does. But he thought Wittgenstein no longer saw philosophy as solving problems, but instead merely as completing puzzles and trivial confusions arising from our thought and talk about the world. Wittgensteinian philosophy, Popper believed, had turned away from investigating the real world in favor of merely investigating language.

> "The earlier Wittgenstein was a man addicted to passionately intense thinking, profoundly aware of difficult problems of which I, like him, felt the importance, and possessed (or at least so I thought) of true philosophical genius. The later Wittgenstein, on the contrary, seems to have grown tired of serious thinking, and to have invented a doctrine which would make such an activity unnecessary."
> —— Bertrand Russell, *My Philosophical Development*

Responses

Since *Philosophical Investigations* was published after his death,

Wittgenstein never had the opportunity to respond to critics of the completed work. Even before publication, although he was active as a teacher at the University of Cambridge, Wittgenstein wrote in isolation and did not often discuss his work as it developed. Unlike most academics, he did not present his work-in-progress to professional colleagues or at conferences. Nor, with one exception[3]—the article, "Some Remarks on Logical Form"—did he publish articles in academic journals.

Instead, the task of defending and developing Wittgenstein's ideas fell to a new generation of philosophers who were profoundly influenced by his thought. Many of these philosophers had been his students at Cambridge University or knew him personally there. Wittgenstein named some of them—Elizabeth Anscombe,* Rush Rhees,* and G. H. von Wright*—as his literary administrators, responsible for the preparation of *Investigations* for publication. The work of philosophers Norman Malcolm* and Peter Geach,* who was also a student of Wittgenstein, shows his profound influence.

One important point that these thinkers made was that Wittgensteinian methods and ideas could be usefully applied to traditional philosophical concerns. They addressed issues that Wittgenstein had never grappled with himself and, in doing so, showed that Wittgenstein's influence could actually be seen as enriching the philosophical tradition rather than undermining it.

Elizabeth Anscombe, for example, wrote important work on the philosophy of action and ethics* where Wittgenstein's influence was apparent. Particularly noteworthy were her book *Intention*[4] and her article "Modern Moral Philosophy."[5] Peter Geach's book, *Mental Acts*,[6] brought a Wittgensteinian perspective to the philosophy of mind. And Norman Malcolm addressed issues in epistemology* (the theory of knowledge), including the problem of skepticism.*[7]

Conflict and Consensus

In the decades since the publication of *Philosophical Investigations*, those for and against Wittgenstein's ideas have engaged in a lively debate about a number of key issues. One concerns the nature of philosophy and its relation to science. Philosophical naturalists*—who say that science and philosophy should comprise a single intellectual enterprise, and that philosophical problems can and should be tackled using the methods of science—oppose Wittgenstein views and those of his supporters. Many metaphysical* philosophers also believe, in contrast to Wittgenstein, that part of the role of philosophy is to construct explanatory theories of the world.

A second area of debate focuses on the philosophy of language. Wittgensteinians have criticized the theory that evaluates the meanings of sentences in a language like English in terms of the conditions under which the sentence counts as true. They believe that what is important in determining meaning is not so much the truth conditions of a sentence, but rather the uses to which the sentences are put.

The third area of debate involves the philosophy of mind. Wittgensteinians and their opponents have disagreed about whether we can meaningfully speak of private experiences.* Private experiences, if they exist, are feelings or sensations that belong only to a particular individual and that cannot be adequately described in language or be known or understood by others.

Philosophers are still arguing about all these issues, and Wittgenstein's followers continue to contribute to the debates.

---

1. Bertrand Russell, *My Philosophical Development* (London: Allen and Unwin, 1959), 216–7.
2. Karl Popper, *Conjectures and Refutations* (London: Routledge, 2002), 92–3.
3. Ludwig Wittgenstein, "Some Remarks on Logical Form," *Proceedings of the Aristotelian Society*, Supplementary Volume 9 (1929): 162–71.
4. Elizabeth Anscombe, *Intention* (Oxford: Blackwell, 1958).
5. Elizabeth Anscombe, "Modern Moral Philosophy," *Philosophy* 33 (1958): 1–19.
6. Peter Geach, *Mental Acts: Their Content and their Objects* (London: Routledge, 1957).
7. Norman Malcolm, *Dreaming* (London: Routledge, 1959).

MODULE 10
THE EVOLVING DEBATE

KEY POINTS

* *Philosophical Investigations* encouraged a focus in the philosophy of language on the different ways in which language can be used in practical, everyday situations.
* The work gave rise to a school of Wittgensteinian thinkers. They applied Wittgenstein's methods and ideas to areas of philosophy that Wittgenstein himself never covered in detail, including ethics, the philosophy of religion, and many areas of the theory of knowledge.
* Contemporary thinkers are still using Wittgensteinian methods and ideas to explore language and the mind.

Uses and Problems

Wittgenstein introduced a new emphasis on ordinary language and the use of linguistic expressions in specific situations. Previous philosophers of language, such as Gottlob Frege,* had often written as if meaning were based in the expressions of the language itself, divorced from the circumstances in which it was used.

Many contemporary philosophers believe in the possibility of constructing a theory of meaning for language. Such a theory would tell us how *facts* about the meanings of expressions in a language determine what speakers mean. Major figures such as Donald Davidson,* Michael Dummett,* and David Kaplan* have supported this approach.

Simply put, the Wittgensteinian challenge to this idea stems from the vital importance of context in understanding utterances. What speakers know merely by virtue of knowing a language is not a strong enough basis for an understanding of actual utterances. To truly comprehend what is being said, you need to know, too, the social context, as well as the speaker's purposes and intentions.

Philosophers interested in constructing theories of meaning for languages have had to account for the importance of context—a point repeatedly emphasized by Wittgenstein. One response to this issue dates back to the work of British language philosopher Paul Grice* in the 1950s and 1960s. This response is still popular today and involves distinguishing semantics* from pragmatics* and seeing them as two distinct and separate parts of linguistics.

Semantics examines what speakers know by virtue of knowing a language. However, this is not to understand what people say in everyday conversation. People can use the same expression to mean different things in different contexts. However, despite two possible meanings, we are usually able to grasp what they mean. Pragmatics studies the knowledge and skills that allow us to do this.

American philosopher David Kaplan,[1] for example, has distinguished between "character" and "content"—meaning the character of a sentence is constant, but its content alters in different circumstances. Similarly, contextualists* in linguistics have attempted to formulate theories to explain the absolute importance of context to understanding.

> "What we are supplying are really remarks on the natural history of human beings; we are not contributing curiosities however, but observations which no one has doubted, but which have escaped remark only because they are always before our eyes."
> ——Ludwig Wittgenstein, *Philosophical Investigations*

Schools of Thought

From the 1960s on, a new generation of Wittgensteinian philosophers emerged. These thinkers, by and large, had not had significant personal contact with Wittgenstein, but had been inspired by reading his works, especially *Philosophical Investigations*. Many members of this group were based in the United States, rather than in Britain, and included Stanley Cavell* and Cora Diamond.*

There were many areas of traditional philosophy that Wittgenstein did not explicitly address in *Investigations*. One of the contributions of the Wittgensteinian philosophers mentioned above is that they extended his insights into topics that he himself had never, or rarely, mentioned. For example, *Investigations* and, in fact, the rest of Wittgenstein's work, include very little discussion of ethics*. Yet Diamond and others have approached ethics from a Wittgensteinian point of view, emphasizing how ethical concepts, like good or virtue, are used in ordinary human life and discourse.

Similarly, early readers of *Investigations* might have thought that traditional epistemology,* the theory of knowledge, was simply not possible in a Wittgensteinian context. Questions of language and meaning, they might assume, simply replace questions of how knowledge is possible. However, thinkers such as Thompson Clarke* and Stanley Cavell* showed that epistemological problems still arise. They also demonstrated how the ideas in *Investigations* shed light on epistemology.

In particular, these thinkers have used Wittgenstein's ideas to explore the old problem of skepticism.* The skeptic says that genuine, objective knowledge of the world is not possible. Traditionally, epistemologists have been concerned with this challenge to the possibility of knowledge and have set out to prove the skeptic wrong. Clarke, Cavell and others have explored what skepticism means and in what senses it can or cannot be proved or disproved.[2]

In Current Scholarship

Today, philosophers like Robert Brandom* and John McDowell* approach philosophical problems in a distinctively Wittgensteinian way—although they disagree on many important philosophical issues.

Wittgenstein himself criticized the construction of grand theories in philosophy and urged philosophers to adopt a piecemeal approach to their work. However, not all of his disciples have followed this advice. Robert Brandom, for instance, is engaged in the construction of a methodical theory of linguistic meaning, sometimes called "inferential role semantics."* Brandom sees Wittgenstein as an inspiration in this project. To simplify a little, Brandom regards the meaning of a linguistic expression as fixed by the *way* it is used, and he connects this with the Wittgensteinian slogan that "meaning is use."

Other followers have rejected this highly theoretical approach and prefer to continue in Wittgenstein's footsteps by looking to get rid of confusions, rather than constructing theories. One of the most influential people using this approach is the British philosopher John McDowell, especially since the publication in 1994 of his influential work, *Mind and World*.[3]

McDowell, like other Wittgensteinians, denies the possibility of what he calls a "sideways on" view of language and mind. We cannot do justice to the mind without using the correct terminology, he contends. We cannot, for example, describe mental phenomena in purely neuroscientific* terms, merely studying the nervous system and particularly the brain. If we do, we will miss some crucial aspects of mind. We cannot understand the mind without considering the ways we describe and make sense of each other in everyday life.

---

1. David Kaplan, "Demonstratives," in *Themes from Kaplan,* ed. Joseph Almog et al (Oxford: Oxford University Press, 1989).
2. Thompson Clarke, "The Legacy of Skepticism," *Journal of Philosophy* 64 (1972): 754–69; Stanley Cavell, *The Claim of Reason* (Oxford: Oxford University Press, 1979).
3. John McDowell, *Mind and World* (Cambridge, Mass.: Harvard University Press, 1994).

MODULE 11
IMPACT AND INFLUENCE TODAY

KEY POINTS

* Scholars and others still widely study *Philosophical Investigations*, and we can see its influence in the work of many contemporary philosophers. However, it is probably less influential than it was in the 1950s and 1960s.
* The book challenges representationalism—the idea that mental states function by representing the way the world is.
* Philosophers have responded, in part, by integrating their views on traditional philosophical issues with contemporary scientific knowledge.

Position

Within the philosophical community, people do not agree on the value and significance of *Philosophical Investigations*. But it is probably true to say that the book has less of an impact today than it did in the 1950s and 1960s. Metaphysics,* under the influence of philosophers such as Saul Kripke* and David Lewis,* has become the principal contemporary focus and goes against the spirit of *Investigations*. Metaphysics concentrates on theorizing about the nature of the world itself, rather than on how we understand it.

Overall, many present-day analytical philosophers, looking at connections between philosophy and science through language, do not think questions of language are as central to philosophy as Wittgenstein and his contemporaries did in the middle of the twentieth century. It remains to be seen, however, whether this is a temporary trend or a permanent state of affairs.

Early critics of the book concentrated on its lessons for the philosophy of mind. In particular, Wittgenstein's "private language argument"* seemed to suggest that one could not speak meaningfully of a person's private sensations. That led to the interpretation of Wittgenstein as a sort of behaviorist*—that is, as saying that the meaning of a sentence like, "Paul is in pain," is to be understood in terms of Paul's external behavior rather than his inner sensations.

After the publication of Kripke's *Wittgenstein on Rules and Private Language* in 1982,[1] the focus shifted greatly to Wittgenstein's views on the philosophy of language. Critics have disputed Kripke's interpretation of Wittgenstein, and most would probably question its accuracy, but he did spark a new debate on how Wittgenstein's ideas can be applied to contemporary discussions about meaning.

> "We all stand, or should stand, in the shadow of Wittgenstein, in the same way that much earlier generations once stood in the shadow of Kant..."
> —— Michael Dummett*, *The Logical Basis of Metaphysics*

Interaction

Philosophical Investigations challenged the dominant view in the philosophy of mind, sometimes called representationalism,* a view also accepted in much of theoretical psychology and cognitive science*, the interdisciplinary study of the mind. Representationalists believe that mental states work by representing the world. They have truth conditions: they state that the world is a certain way. Wittgenstein implicitly questions this model of understanding the mind in *Investigations*. He suggests representation turns out to be a very particular notion, one that has a legitimate use, but is not applicable to all mental states.

More broadly, Wittgenstein's work contrasts what science and philosophy actually do. One of his themes is the idea that scientists should be engaged in the task of constructing theories, but philosophers should not. The role of philosophy is to clear up confusions rather than add to our theoretical knowledge of the world. This challenges the way that philosophers have traditionally seen their discipline.

Critics inspired by Wittgenstein's writings have advanced these challenges to mainstream philosophy. It is a matter of controversy, however, as to how true such critics are to the intentions of Wittgenstein himself. The correct interpretation of his philosophy is still a matter of debate.

The Continuing Debate

Defenders of representationalism in the philosophy of mind have modified their views in order to take account of Wittgensteinian criticisms. Representationalists describe the mind as representing or reflecting the world, or as stating that the world is a certain way. Much recent debate has focused on the issue of perception. On this point, representationalists believe that seeing an apple on a table involves forming a mental picture (representation) of an apple on a table.

In the past, that view was often assumed rather than asserted and defended. Partly due to the pressure of Wittgensteinian criticisms, recent supporters of this view have begun to formulate arguments to back up their claim. They have also examined more closely the issue of precisely what perceptual representations are. The philosopher Susanna Siegel,* for example, has examined these issues with the intention of strengthening the defenses of representationalism against these criticisms.

While these responses to Wittgenstein's arguments do not necessarily come from a single philosophical perspective, it is possible to identify a common theme. Representationalism in philosophy of mind is essentially a naturalistic* movement. It happily connects the philosophy of mind with developments in cognitive science* and empirical psychology. This is a similar approach to that of the philosophy of language mentioned above—attempting to address issues of meaning in a scientific manner.

Collectively, then, these philosophers are trying to reintegrate philosophy and science, disciplines that Wittgenstein believed to be quite separate. They are advocates of a more scientific world view than Wittgenstein thought possible or desirable.

---

1. Saul Kripke, *Wittgenstein on Rules and Private Language* (Oxford: Blackwell, 1982).

MODULE 12
WHERE NEXT?

KEY POINTS

* Contextualists* in philosophy of language and in epistemology (the philosophy of knowledge) continue to draw inspiration from Wittgenstein's ideas.
* *Philosophical Investigations* emphasizes the importance of the human in determining meaning.
* *Investigations* is a complex text with implications for many areas of philosophy. It will continue to be a source of inspiration and disagreement.

Potential

Ludwig Wittgenstein's *Philosophical Investigations* is probably less influential today than it was in the first 20 years after its publication. However, it is still very widely read and studied. Two recently popular philosophical views that have some affinities with Wittgenstein's arguments may affect its future influence. Both these views are frequently known as "contextualism:"* one in the philosophy of language and the other in epistemology,* the theory of knowledge.

In the philosophy of language, contextualism is the view that the meaning of what someone says is profoundly affected by its context. When I say a sentence in English, its meaning is not determined by facts about English. To discover what it means, we must look at the situation in which I spoke. Arguably, this is a view that Wittgenstein puts forward in *Philosophical Investigations*.

Certainly, the contemporary supporters of this argument draw inspiration from Wittgenstein's views.

In epistemology, contextualism is the view that what counts as knowledge in one context may not count as knowledge in another. I may believe I know, for everyday purposes, that a colleague is trustworthy. But if I am a witness in a court of law, where higher standards of evidence are demanded, I may not count on knowing this. Wittgenstein put forward something like this view in his late work *On Certainty*, but it also has roots in *Investigations*.

> "For Wittgenstein, philosophy comes to grief not in denying what we all know to be true, but in its effort to escape those human forms of life which alone provide the coherence of our expression. He wishes an acknowledgement of human limitation which does not leave us chafed by our own skin, by a sense of powerlessness to penetrate beyond the human conditions of knowledge."
>
> —— Stanley Cavell, *The Availability of Wittgenstein's Later Philosophy*

Future Directions

Some influential contemporary thinkers, such as the American philosopher Charles Travis,* have drawn inspiration from Wittgenstein in arguing for forms of contextualism in the philosophy of language. Travis calls for a very radical form of contextualism. In his books *The Uses of Sense*[1] and *Thought's Footing*,[2] he draws on *Investigations* and Wittgenstein's other late writings to support his argument that the context in which language is used has a very deep and extensive role in determining meaning.

Another American philosopher, Michael Williams,* has used Wittgenstein's writings to argue for contextualism in epistemology, especially in his book *Unnatural Doubts*.³ Williams claims that certain concepts in Wittgenstein's work undermine skepticism:* the view that genuine knowledge of the world is impossible. Skeptics have argued, for example, that I cannot truly know that there is a cup on my desk because it is possible that I am merely dreaming or hallucinating the presence of a cup.

Williams argues that skeptical doubts do not always need to be taken seriously. Doubts arise in particular contexts: when, for example, I have particular reason to suppose that things are not as they seem. Wittgenstein's lesson here, as always, is that meaning depends on context. Doubts may make sense in one context, but not in another.

Summary

Wittgenstein's *Philosophical Investigations* was a crucially important text in the development of analytical philosophy* in the twentieth century. It revolutionized the philosophy of language by paying previously unheard of attention to ordinary language. It revealed the true complexity of such language and so began a move away from the formal models of language that philosophers had used in the past.

His work also drew attention to the diversity and complexity of debates about the human mind providing a fresh impetus for the philosophy of mind, which has been in the centre of philosophical reasearch ever since. It raised crucial questions, too, about the nature and everyday workings of philosophy itself: how much can philosophy achieve and how much should it attempt to achieve?

This is a very rich book. It continues to be a source of new ideas and inspiration for philosophers and students, and its ideas have by no means been exhausted. And while its unusual style makes it difficult to master (a long series of related remarks rather than a continuous argument), it has proven very important in inspiring new and original work by philosophers.

To summarize the significance of the work, you might say that it marked a return to an emphasis on the role of the human. Notions crucial to philosophy like truth, meaning, and representation are not abstractions remote from human experience, Wittgenstein said, but can be understood by examining the human contexts in which they are actually used.

Wittgenstein can be regarded as a kind of naturalist,* even though he is often seen as anti-naturalist. Why? Because he opposed the view that the natural sciences can ultimately solve all intellectual problems, including philosophical ones. But he is a naturalist in a broader sense, believing that the ideas that create philosophical problems do not transcend human experience, but are part of it and find their meaning in their use in life.

Perhaps, then, the future importance of *Philosophical Investigations* will lie in acknowledgement of the human origins of all the words and concepts that affect abstract philosophical problems.

1. Charles Travis, *The Uses of Sense: Wittgenstein's Philosophy of Language* (Oxford: Clarendon, 1989).
2. Charles Travis, *Thought's Footing* (Oxford: Oxford University Press, 2006).
3. Michael Williams, *Unnatural Doubts: Epistemological Realism and the Basis of Scepticism* (Oxford: Blackwell, 1991).

GLOSSARY OF TERMS

1. **Analytical philosophy:** an influential twentieth-century philosophical movement—associated particularly with Britain, Germany, and the United States—that emphasized logic, language, and the connections between philosophy and science.
2. **Anthropology:** the scientific study of human beings and culture.
3. **Aspect perception:** the phenomenon whereby the same object can be perceived in different ways. A drawing, for example, may be perceived either as a picture of a duck or a picture of a rabbit.
4. **Behaviorism:** the view that mental states should be understood in terms of behavior—for example, that being angry is essentially a matter of behaving in an angry fashion.
5. **Cognitive science:** the interdisciplinary study of the mind, encompassing parts of psychology, philosophy, linguistics, and computer science.
6. **Conceptual analysis:** a philosophical method using the analysis of words and concepts to discover their meanings.
7. **Contextualism:** the view that the meaning of a word or sentence is dependent on the context in which the word or sentence is used.
8. **Empiricism:** the view that all human knowledge comes from experience.
9. **Epistemology:** a branch of philosophy dealing with knowledge.
10. **Ethics:** a branch of philosophy dealing with morality and what is good.
11. **Fideism:** the view that religious belief is based in faith rather than reason.
12. **Gestalt school:** a school of psychologists prominent in Germany and Austria in the early twentieth century that advocated that perception should be understood in an integrated manner. Its leading figure was perhaps Wolfgang Köhler (1887–1967).
13. **Inferential role semantics:** the view that the meaning of an expression should be understood in terms of its inferential roles with other expressions, rather than its truth conditions.

14. **Intentionality:** the object-directedness or "aboutness" of a state. Fear is intentional, for example, insofar as it is fear *of* something.
15. **Language games:** a simple scenario in which speakers use words or sentences for particular purposes and according to definite rules.
16. **Logic:** a branch of mathematics and philosophy dealing with reasoning in general and inference in particular.
17. **Logical atomism:** the philosophical view that all meaningful sentences are constructed logically from basic or atomic sentences about simple objects or logical atoms.
18. **Logical positivism:** a radical philosophical movement—active from the late 1920s, especially in Austria and Germany—that emphasizes the logical analysis of language.
19. **Mental entity:** something that exists in the mind, arguably including ideas, thoughts, feelings and experiences.
20. **Metaphysics:** a branch of philosophy dealing with the ultimate or fundamental constituents of reality, with what there fundamentally is.
21. **Modernism:** a movement in literature, music, art, and architecture, particularly in the early twentieth century, characterized by a decisive break with tradition.
22. **Naturalism:** in philosophy, the view that philosophy and science are engaged in the same project and use essentially the same methods.
23. **Neuroscience:** the scientific study of the nervous system, including the brain.
24. **Ordinary language philosophy:** a school of philosophy associated particularly with the University of Oxford in the 1950s and 1960s, emphasizing careful attention to language use.
25. **Philosophy as therapy:** philosophical writing aimed at removing intellectual problems and confusions rather than arriving at new truths about the world.
26. **Pragmatics:** the study of the rules and conventions that govern the use of

language.

27. **Private experience:** an experience that cannot be adequately described in language and can therefore only be understood by the person who has the experience.

28. **Private language:** a language that can be understood only by one person.

29. **Representationalism:** the view that language and mind function primarily by representing the world accurately or inaccurately.

30. **Skepticism:** the view that genuine knowledge of the world is impossible.

31. **Scientism:** the view that all-important intellectual questions can be answered by the methods of science.

32. **Semantics:** the study of linguistic meaning.

33. **Sense data:** mental entities that some philosophers think are the direct objects of perceptual experience. It is sometimes believed, for example, that the direct objects of vision are color patches, or that the direct objects of hearing are sounds.

34. **Sociology:** the scientific study of society.

35. **Theology:** the study of the nature of God and God's attributes.

36. **World War I (1914–1918):** a major conflict involving all of the main European powers (primarily Germany, France, and Great Britain) and a number of other world powers, including the United States and Japan.

 # PEOPLE MENTIONED IN THE TEXT

1. **Elizabeth Anscombe (1919–2001)** was a British philosopher. A student of Wittgenstein's, she became perhaps the leading Wittgensteinian philosopher of the post-war period.

2. **John L. Austin (1911–60)** was a British philosopher and a leader of the so-called "ordinary language" school of philosophy. He made major contributions to both the philosophy of language and the philosophy of perception.

3. **Alain Badiou (b. 1937)** is a French philosopher. He has written on metaphysics and set theory.

4. **Ludwig van Beethoven (1770–1827)** was a German composer. His symphonic and chamber works are frequently regarded as forming a bridge between the classical and romantic musical eras.

5. **David Bloor (b. 1942)** is a British sociologist. He is best known as a founder of the "Edinburgh school," which seeks to understand science in sociological terms.

6. **Jacques Bouveresse (b. 1940)** is a French philosopher. He has defended and developed analytical philosophy in a style more usually associated with the English-speaking world.

7. **Robert Brandom (b. 1950)** is an American philosopher. He has written widely on the philosophy of language and mind, as well as the history of philosophy.

8. **Rudolph Carnap (1891–1970)** was a German philosopher and leader of the logical positivist movement. He contributed to logic, the philosophy of language and the philosophy of science.

9. **Stanley Cavell (b. 1926)** is an American philosopher. He has written widely on Wittgenstein, philosophy, and the arts, particularly cinema.

10. **Thompson Clarke (1928–2012)** was an American philosopher. Although he published only two short articles, Clarke was influential in epistemology.

11. **Nicolaus Copernicus (1473–1543)** was a Polish astronomer and mathematician.

He advocated heliocentrism, according to which the sun and not the earth is at the center of the solar system.

12. **Donald Davidson (1917–2003)** was an American philosopher of language. His writings on philosophy of language and philosophy of mind became highly influential from the 1970s.

13. **Cora Diamond (b. 1937)** is an American philosopher. She has written widely on ethics, philosophy of language, and Wittgenstein.

14. **Michael Dummett (1925–2011)** was a British philosopher. He was both an influential philosopher of language in his own right and the leading interpreter of the works of Frege.

15. **Gottlob Frege (1848–1925)** was a German mathematician and philosopher. Though little known during his lifetime, his work in logic and the philosophy of language later revolutionized those subjects.

16. **Sigmund Freud (1856–1939)** was a German psychologist and the founder of psychoanalysis. He suggested that a system of unconscious drives and repressions determines much of human behavior.

17. **Peter Geach (1916–2013)** was a British philosopher. He wrote widely on logic, language, and the history of philosophy.

18. **H. P. Grice (1913–88)** was a British philosopher of language. He is considered an important figure in both philosophy and linguistics and a founder of the discipline of pragmatics.

19. **Peter Hacker (b. 1939)** is a British philosopher. He is one of the foremost interpreters of Wittgenstein's work.

20. **Martin Heidegger (1889–1976)** was a German philosopher. He is associated with the phenomenological school, which flourished in Germany and France in the early twentieth century and aimed to study consciousness from the subjective, first person point of view.

21. **Derek Jarman (1942–94)** was an English filmmaker. He is known for his experimental film style and for tackling controversial topics.

22. **Immanuel Kant (1724–1804)** was a German philosopher. He was the author of *The Critique of Pure Reason* (1781) and perhaps the most influential philosopher of the modern era.

23. **David Kaplan (b. 1933)** is an American philosopher. He has contributed important ideas to the philosophy of language.

24. **Gustav Klimt (1862–1918)** was an Austrian painter. His work is marked by an unconventional style and frank eroticism.

25. **Saul Kripke (b. 1940)** is an American philosopher. He has contributed to logic, philosophy of language, and numerous other fields, and he is widely regarded as one of the most important contemporary philosophers.

26. **Thomas Kuhn (1922–96)** was an American philosopher and historian of science. He is best known for emphasizing the importance of historical conditions in the formation of scientific knowledge.

27. **John McDowell (b. 1942)** is a British philosopher. He has written on many topics, including Aristotle, ethics, epistemology, and the philosophy of mind.

28. **Norman Malcolm (1911–90)** was an American philosopher. He contributed to epistemology and was one of the first generation of Wittgenstein scholars in the United States.

29. **Wolfgang Amadeus Mozart (1756–91)** was an Austrian composer. His symphonies, masses, operas, and concertos are considered central works of the classical era of music.

30. **Kai Nielsen (b. 1926)** is a Canadian philosopher. He has written widely on the philosophy of religion.

31. **D. Z. Phillips (1934–2006)** was a Welsh philosopher. Profoundly influenced by Wittgenstein, he wrote widely on ethics, literature, and religion.

32. **Karl Popper (1902–94)** was an Austrian philosopher. He is one of the best-known philosophers of science of the twentieth century.

33. **Frank Ramsey (1903–30)** was an English philosopher, economist, and

mathematician. He was one of the first commentators on Wittgenstein's works and assisted in the first English translation of the *Tractatus Logico-Philosophicus*.

34. **Rush Rhees (1905–89)** was a British philosopher. He applied Wittgensteinian ideas to the philosophy of religion.

35. **I. A. Richards (1893–1979)** was an English literary critic. He wrote poetry as well as influential works of literary theory.

36. **Richard Rorty (1931–2007)** was an American philosopher. He was a radical critic of contemporary philosophical trends and wrote widely on literature as well as the philosophy of language.

37. **Bertrand Russell (1872–1970)** was a British philosopher, logician, social commentator, and political activist. His early work on logic and the basics of mathematics helped to lay the foundations of analytical philosophy.

38. **Gilbert Ryle (1900–76)** was a leading British philosopher. Often associated with the so-called "ordinary language" school, his most important contributions were to the philosophy of mind.

39. **Arnold Schoenberg (1874–1951)** was an Austrian composer. His music was revolutionary, particularly because of his break with traditional harmony.

40. **Franz Schubert (1797–1828)** was an Austrian composer. His many symphonic and chamber works and songs are regarded as major examples of early romantic music.

41. **John Searle (b. 1932)** is an American philosopher. He has contributed both to the philosophy of language and the philosophy of mind.

42. **Susanna Siegel** is an American philosopher who is currently the Edgar Pierce Professor of Philosophy at Harvard University. Her main focus is on epistemology and the philosophy of mind.

43. **Charles Travis (b. 1943)** is an American philosopher. He is a noted advocate of radical contextualism in the philosophy of language.

44. **David Foster Wallace (1962–2008)** was an American writer. He is known for his novels and also his nonfiction work.
45. **Alfred North Whitehead (1861–1947)** was a British mathematician and philosopher. He is known both for his foundational work in mathematical logic and his work in metaphysics.
46. **Michael Williams (b. 1947)** is an American philosopher. He has written widely on epistemology and on Wittgenstein.
47. **Georg Henrik von Wright (1916–2003)** was a Finnish philosopher. He wrote widely on logic and the philosophy of language.

WORKS CITED

1. Anscombe, Elizabeth. *Intention.* Oxford: Blackwell, 1958.
2. ——. "Modern Moral Philosophy," *Philosophy* 33, no. 124 (1958): 1–19.
3. Badiou, Alain. *Being and Event.* London: Continuum, 2005.
4. Bloor, David. *Wittgenstein, Rules and Institutions.* London: Routledge, 1997.
5. Braver, Lee. *Groundless Grounds: a Study of Wittgenstein and Heidegger.* Cambridge, Mass.: MIT Press, 2012.
6. Cavell, Stanley. *The Claim of Reason.* Oxford: Oxford University Press, 1979.
7. Clarke, Thompson. "The Legacy of Skepticism," *Journal of Philosophy* 64 (1972), pp. 754–69.
8. Dummett, Michael. *Truth and Other Enigmas.* London: Duckworth, 1978.
9. Frege, Gottlob. *Foundations of Arithmetic.* Translated by J. L. Austin. Oxford: Blackwell, 1950.
10. Geach, Peter. *Mental Acts: their Content and their Objects.* London: Routledge, 1957.
11. Guetti, James. *Wittgenstein and the Grammar of Literary Experience.* Athens GA: University of Georgia Press, 1993.
12. Hacker, Peter. *Insight and Illusion.* Oxford: Clarendon Press, 1972.
13. ——. *Wittgenstein: Connections and Controversies.* Oxford: Oxford University Press, 2013.
14. Horwich, Paul. *Wittgenstein's Metaphilosophy.* Oxford: Oxford University Press, 2013.
15. Kaplan, David. "Demonstratives," *Themes from Kaplan.* Edited by Joseph Almog, John Perry and Howard Wettstein. Oxford: Oxford University Press, 1989.
16. Kerr, Fergus. *Theology after Wittgenstein.* Oxford: Blackwell, 1986.
17. Kripke, Saul. *Naming and Necessity.* Oxford: Blackwell, 1980.
18. ——. *Wittgenstein on Rules and Private Language.* Oxford: Blackwell, 1982.
19. Kuhn, Thomas. *The Structure of Scientific Revolutions.* Chicago: University of Chicago Press, 1962.
20. Malcolm, Norman. *Dreaming.* London: Routledge and Kegan Paul, 1959.

21. Monk, Ray. *Ludwig Wittgenstein: the Duty of Genius*. London: Vintage, 1991.
22. Moyal-Sharrock, Daniel, ed. *The Third Wittgenstein*. Aldershot: Ashgate, 2004.
23. McDowell, John. *Mind and World*. Cambridge, Mass.: Harvard University Press, 1994.
24. Neilsen, Kai and D. Z. Phillips. *Wittgensteinian Fideism?* London: SCM Press, 2005.
25. Pears, David. *Wittgenstein*. London: Fontana, 1971.
26. Popper, Karl. *Conjectures and Refutations: the Growth of Scientific Knowledge*. London: Routledge, 2002.
27. Read, Rupert and Crary, Alice. *The New Wittgenstein*. London: Routledge, 2000.
28. Rorty, Richard. *Philosophy and the Mirror of Nature*. Princeton: Princeton University Press, 1979.
29. Russell, Bertrand. *The Principles of Mathematics*. London: Allen and Unwin, 1903.
30. ———. *The Philosophy of Logical Atomism*. London: Routledge, 2009.
31. ———. "On Denoting," *Mind* 14 (1905): 479–93.
32. ———. *My Philosophical Development*. London: Allen and Unwin, 1959.
33. Russell, Bertrand, and Alfred North Whitehead. *Principia Mathematica*. Cambridge: Cambridge University Press, 1910–13.
34. Searle, John. "Proper names," *Mind* 67 (1958): 166–73.
35. Travis, Charles. *Thought's Footing*. Oxford: Oxford University Press, 2006.
36. ———. *The Uses of Sense: Wittgenstein's Philosophy of Language*. Oxford: Clarendon, 1989.
37. Williams, Michael. *Unnatural Doubts: Epistemological Realism and the Basis of Scepticism*. Oxford: Blackwell, 1991.
38. Williamson, Timothy. *The Philosophy of Philosophy*. Oxford: Blackwell, 2007.
39. Wittgenstein, Ludwig. *Philosophical Investigations*. Translated by Elizabeth Anscombe. Oxford: Blackwell, 2001.
40. ———. *The Blue and Brown Books*. Oxford: Blackwell, 1958.
41. ———. *On Certainty*. Translated by Denis Paul and G. E. M. Anscombe. Oxford:

Blackwell, 1969.

42. ——. *Philosophical Grammar*. Edited by Rush Rhees. Translated by Anthony Kenny. Oxford: Blackwell, 1974.

43. ——. *Philosophical Remarks*. Edited by Rush Rhees. Translated by Raymond Hargreaves and Roger White. Oxford: Blackwell, 1975.

44. ——. *Remarks on the Philosophy of Psychology*. Vol. 1. Edited by G. E. M. Anscombe and G. H. von Wright. Translated by G. E. M. Anscombe. Oxford: Blackwell, 1980.

45. ——. *Remarks on the Philosophy of Psychology*. Vol. 2. Edited by G. H. von Wright and Heikki Nyman. Translated by C. G. Luckhardt and M. A. E. Aue. Oxford: Blackwell, 1980.

46. ——. *Tractatus Logico-Philosophicus*. Translated by David Pears and Brian McGuinness. London: Routledge and Kegan Paul, 1974.

47. ——. *Lectures and Conversations on Aesthetics, Philosophy and Religious Belief*. Edited by Cyril Barrett. Oxford: Blackwell, 1967.

48. ——. *Wittgenstein in Cambridge: Letters and Documents 1911–1951*. Edited by Brian McGuinness. Malden MA: Blackwell, 2008.

49. ——. "Some Remarks on Logical Form," *Proceedings of the Aristotelian Society*, Supplementary Volume 9 (1929), 162–71.

原书作者简介

奥地利哲学家路德维希·维特根斯坦1889年出生于维也纳的一个豪门望族。他最初立志成为一名工程师，在英格兰的曼彻斯特大学求学期间，他对数学哲学产生了兴趣，进而又将兴趣推广到了哲学。

一战时，维特根斯坦加入了奥地利军队，并在战场上完成了他的第一部重要著作。他曾一度放弃哲学，但又重返哲学舞台并最终在剑桥大学执教。在经历了一场与癌症病魔的搏斗后，他于1951年逝世。

本书作者简介

迈克尔·奥沙利文博士为伦敦国王学院哲学系助教，《维特根斯坦与感知》一书的主编。

世界名著中的批判性思维

《世界思想宝库钥匙丛书》致力于深入浅出地阐释全世界著名思想家的观点，不论是谁、在何处都能了解到，从而推进批判性思维发展。

《世界思想宝库钥匙丛书》与世界顶尖大学的一流学者合作，为一系列学科中最有影响的著作推出新的分析文本，介绍其观点和影响。在这一不断扩展的系列中，每种选入的著作都代表了历经时间考验的思想典范。通过为这些著作提供必要背景、揭示原作者的学术渊源以及说明这些著作所产生的影响，本系列图书希望让读者以新视角看待这些划时代的经典之作。读者应学会思考、运用并挑战这些著作中的观点，而不是简单接受它们。

ABOUT THE AUTHOR OF THE ORIGINAL WORK

Austrian philosopher **Ludwig Wittgenstein** was born into a hugely wealthy Viennese family in 1889. Originally destined to be an engineer, he became interested in the philosophy of mathematics and then philosophy generally while a student at Manchester University in England.

Wittgenstein fought in the Austrian Army in World War I and wrote his first important work while a soldier. He gave up philosophy for a while, but returned to it and eventually taught at Cambridge University. He died, after a battle with cancer, in 1951.

ABOUT THE AUTHORS OF THE ANALYSIS

Dr Michael O'Sullivan is a tutor in the Department of Philosophy, King's College London. He is the editor of *Wittgenstein and Perception*.

ABOUT MACAT
GREAT WORKS FOR CRITICAL THINKING

Macat is focused on making the ideas of the world's great thinkers accessible and comprehensible to everybody, everywhere, in ways that promote the development of enhanced critical thinking skills.

It works with leading academics from the world's top universities to produce new analyses that focus on the ideas and the impact of the most influential works ever written across a wide variety of academic disciplines. Each of the works that sit at the heart of its growing library is an enduring example of great thinking. But by setting them in context—and looking at the influences that shaped their authors, as well as the responses they provoked—Macat encourages readers to look at these classics and game-changers with fresh eyes. Readers learn to think, engage and challenge their ideas, rather than simply accepting them.

批判性思维与《哲学研究》

首要批判性思维技巧：分析

次要批判性思维技巧：阐释

许多人仍将路德维希·维特根斯坦 1953 年出版的《哲学研究》视为 20 世纪哲学的巨作之一。

该书提出了对于哲学本身的一种崭新的见解，并揭示了精妙的分析性思维的所有特征。维特根斯坦接过了柏拉图的论题，并对之进行了详尽（且十分清晰）的分析，从而对于如何分析与评价一个极为复杂的论题中不同成分的次序与功能提出了自己的理解。由此，他必然站在了一个与柏拉图的哲学既一致又不一致的立场上。

《哲学研究》也是一个展示阐释技巧的极佳范例。哲学问题常常产生于语言使用中的混乱——维特根斯坦料定，解决这些问题的方法乃澄清语言的使用。他主张哲学家们必须研究语言的日常使用，并考察人们如何在日常生活中将语言作为工具使用。依照这一高度阐释性的方法，一个词或一句话的意思便关涉其使用的语境（人、文化、社群）。维特根斯坦敦促哲学家们要关注日常生活和人们身处的具体处境，而不要争论那些抽象的问题。

CRITICAL THINKING AND *PHILOSOPHICAL INVESTIGATIONS*

- Primary critical thinking skill: ANALYSIS
- Secondary critical thinking skill: INTERPRETATION

Many still consider Ludwig Wittgenstein's 1953 *Philosophical Investigations* to be one of the breakthrough works of twentieth-century philosophy.

The book sets out a radically new conception of philosophy itself, and demonstrates all the attributes of a fine analytical mind. Taking an argument from Plato and subjecting it to detailed (and very clear) analysis, Wittgenstein shows his understanding of how the sequence and function of differing parts of a highly-complex argument can be broken down and assessed. In so doing, he reaches a logical position of simultaneous agreement and disagreement with Plato's philosophical position.

Philosophical Investigations is also a powerful example of the skill of interpretation. Philosophical problems often arise from confusions in the use of language—and the way to solve these problems, Wittgenstein posits, is by clarifying language use. He argues that philosophers must study ordinary uses of language and examine how people use it as a tool in their everyday lives. In this highly-interpretative way, the meaning of a word or sentence becomes relative to the context (people, culture, community) in which it is used. Rather than debate abstract problems, WittgensteIn urges philosophers to concern themselves with ordinary life and the concrete situations in which humans find themselves.

《世界思想宝库钥匙丛书》简介

《世界思想宝库钥匙丛书》致力于为一系列在各领域产生重大影响的人文社科类经典著作提供独特的学术探讨。每一本读物都不仅仅是原经典著作的内容摘要,而是介绍并深入研究原经典著作的学术渊源、主要观点和历史影响。这一丛书的目的是提供一套学习资料,以促进读者掌握批判性思维,从而更全面、深刻地去理解重要思想。

每一本读物分为3个部分:学术渊源、学术思想和学术影响,每个部分下有4个小节。这些章节旨在从各个方面研究原经典著作及其反响。

由于独特的体例,每一本读物不但易于阅读,而且另有一项优点:所有读物的编排体例相同,读者在进行某个知识层面的调查或研究时可交叉参阅多本该丛书中的相关读物,从而开启跨领域研究的路径。

为了方便阅读,每本读物最后还列出了术语表和人名表(在书中则以星号*标记),此外还有参考文献。

《世界思想宝库钥匙丛书》与剑桥大学合作,理清了批判性思维的要点,即如何通过6种技能来进行有效思考。其中3种技能让我们能够理解问题,另3种技能让我们有能力解决问题。这6种技能合称为"批判性思维PACIER模式",它们是:

分析:了解如何建立一个观点;
评估:研究一个观点的优点和缺点;
阐释:对意义所产生的问题加以理解;
创造性思维:提出新的见解,发现新的联系;
解决问题:提出切实有效的解决办法;
理性化思维:创建有说服力的观点。

THE MACAT LIBRARY

The Macat Library is a series of unique academic explorations of seminal works in the humanities and social sciences — books and papers that have had a significant and widely recognised impact on their disciplines. It has been created to serve as much more than just a summary of what lies between the covers of a great book. It illuminates and explores the influences on, ideas of, and impact of that book. Our goal is to offer a learning resource that encourages critical thinking and fosters a better, deeper understanding of important ideas.

Each publication is divided into three Sections: Influences, Ideas, and Impact. Each Section has four Modules. These explore every important facet of the work, and the responses to it.

This Section-Module structure makes a Macat Library book easy to use, but it has another important feature. Because each Macat book is written to the same format, it is possible (and encouraged!) to cross-reference multiple Macat books along the same lines of inquiry or research. This allows the reader to open up interesting interdisciplinary pathways.

To further aid your reading, lists of glossary terms and people mentioned are included at the end of this book (these are indicated by an asterisk [*] throughout) — as well as a list of works cited.

Macat has worked with the University of Cambridge to identify the elements of critical thinking and understand the ways in which six different skills combine to enable effective thinking.

Three allow us to fully understand a problem; three more give us the tools to solve it. Together, these six skills make up the PACIER model of critical thinking. They are:

ANALYSIS — understanding how an argument is built
EVALUATION — exploring the strengths and weaknesses of an argument
INTERPRETATION — understanding issues of meaning
CREATIVE THINKING — coming up with new ideas and fresh connections
PROBLEM-SOLVING — producing strong solutions
REASONING — creating strong arguments .

"《世界思想宝库钥匙丛书》提供了独一无二的跨学科学习和研究工具。它介绍那些革新了各自学科研究的经典著作,还邀请全世界一流专家和教育机构进行严谨的分析,为每位读者打开世界顶级教育的大门。"

—— 安德烈亚斯·施莱歇尔,
经济合作与发展组织教育与技能司司长

"《世界思想宝库钥匙丛书》直面大学教育的巨大挑战……他们组建了一支精干而活跃的学者队伍,来推出在研究广度上颇具新意的教学材料。"

—— 布罗尔斯教授、勋爵,剑桥大学前校长

"《世界思想宝库钥匙丛书》的愿景令人赞叹。它通过分析和阐释那些曾深刻影响人类思想以及社会、经济发展的经典文本,提供了新的学习方法。它推动批判性思维,这对于任何社会和经济体来说都是至关重要的。这就是未来的学习方法。"

—— 查尔斯·克拉克阁下,英国前教育大臣

"对于那些影响了各自领域的著作,《世界思想宝库钥匙丛书》能让人们立即了解到围绕那些著作展开的评论性言论,这让该系列图书成为在这些领域从事研究的师生们不可或缺的资源。"

—— 威廉·特朗佐教授,加利福尼亚大学圣地亚哥分校

"Macat offers an amazing first-of-its-kind tool for interdisciplinary learning and research. Its focus on works that transformed their disciplines and its rigorous approach, drawing on the world's leading experts and educational institutions, opens up a world-class education to anyone."

—— Andreas Schleicher, Director for Education and Skills, Organisation for Economic Co-operation and Development

"Macat is taking on some of the major challenges in university education... They have drawn together a strong team of active academics who are producing teaching materials that are novel in the breadth of their approach."

—— Prof Lord Broers, former Vice-Chancellor of the University of Cambridge

"The Macat vision is exceptionally exciting. It focuses upon new modes of learning which analyse and explain seminal texts which have profoundly influenced world thinking and so social and economic development. It promotes the kind of critical thinking which is essential for any society and economy. This is the learning of the future."

—— Rt Hon Charles Clarke, former UK Secretary of State for Education

"The Macat analyses provide immediate access to the critical conversation surrounding the books that have shaped their respective discipline, which will make them an invaluable resource to all of those, students and teachers, working in the field."

—— Prof William Tronzo, University of California at San Diego

The Macat Library
世界思想宝库钥匙丛书

TITLE	中文书名	类别
An Analysis of Arjun Appadurai's *Modernity at Large: Cultural Dimensions of Globalisation*	解析阿尔君·阿帕杜莱《消失的现代性：全球化的文化维度》	人类学
An Analysis of Claude Lévi-Strauss's *Structural Anthropology*	解析克劳德·列维-斯特劳斯《结构人类学》	人类学
An Analysis of Marcel Mauss's *The Gift*	解析马塞尔·莫斯《礼物》	人类学
An Analysis of Jared M. Diamond's *Guns, Germs, and Steel: The Fate of Human Societies*	解析贾雷德·戴蒙德《枪炮、病菌与钢铁：人类社会的命运》	人类学
An Analysis of Clifford Geertz's *The Interpretation of Cultures*	解析克利福德·格尔茨《文化的解释》	人类学
An Analysis of Philippe Ariès's *Centuries of Childhood: A Social History of Family Life*	解析菲力浦·阿利埃斯《儿童的世纪：旧制度下的儿童和家庭生活》	人类学
An Analysis of W. Chan Kim & Renée Mauborgne's *Blue Ocean Strategy*	解析金伟灿/勒妮·莫博涅《蓝海战略》	商业
An Analysis of John P. Kotter's *Leading Change*	解析约翰·P.科特《领导变革》	商业
An Analysis of Michael E. Porter's *Competitive Strategy: Techniques for Analyzing Industries and Competitors*	解析迈克尔·E.波特《竞争战略：分析产业和竞争对手的技术》	商业
An Analysis of Jean Lave & Etienne Wenger's *Situated Learning: Legitimate Peripheral Participation*	解析琼·莱夫/艾蒂纳·温格《情境学习：合法的边缘性参与》	商业
An Analysis of Douglas McGregor's *The Human Side of Enterprise*	解析道格拉斯·麦格雷戈《企业的人性面》	商业
An Analysis of Milton Friedman's *Capitalism and Freedom*	解析米尔顿·弗里德曼《资本主义与自由》	商业
An Analysis of Ludwig von Mises's *The Theory of Money and Credit*	解析路德维希·冯·米塞斯《货币和信用理论》	经济学
An Analysis of Adam Smith's *The Wealth of Nations*	解析亚当·斯密《国富论》	经济学
An Analysis of Thomas Piketty's *Capital in the Twenty-First Century*	解析托马斯·皮凯蒂《21世纪资本论》	经济学
An Analysis of Nassim Nicholas Taleb's *The Black Swan: The Impact of the Highly Improbable*	解析纳西姆·尼古拉斯·塔勒布《黑天鹅：如何应对不可预知的未来》	经济学
An Analysis of Ha-Joon Chang's *Kicking Away the Ladder*	解析张夏准《富国陷阱：发达国家为何踢开梯子》	经济学
An Analysis of Thomas Robert Malthus's *An Essay on the Principle of Population*	解析托马斯·马尔萨斯《人口论》	经济学

An Analysis of John Maynard Keynes's *The General Theory of Employment, Interest and Money*	解析约翰·梅纳德·凯恩斯《就业、利息和货币通论》	经济学
An Analysis of Milton Friedman's *The Role of Monetary Policy*	解析米尔顿·弗里德曼《货币政策的作用》	经济学
An Analysis of Burton G. Malkiel's *A Random Walk Down Wall Street*	解析伯顿·G. 马尔基尔《漫步华尔街》	经济学
An Analysis of Friedrich A. Hayek's *The Road to Serfdom*	解析弗里德里希·A. 哈耶克《通往奴役之路》	经济学
An Analysis of Charles P. Kindleberger's *Manias, Panics, and Crashes: A History of Financial Crises*	解析查尔斯·P. 金德尔伯格《疯狂、惊恐和崩溃：金融危机史》	经济学
An Analysis of Amartya Sen's *Development as Freedom*	解析阿马蒂亚·森《以自由看待发展》	经济学
An Analysis of Rachel Carson's *Silent Spring*	解析蕾切尔·卡森《寂静的春天》	地理学
An Analysis of Charles Darwin's *On the Origin of Species: by Means of Natural Selection, or The Preservation of Favoured Races in the Struggle for Life*	解析查尔斯·达尔文《物种起源》	地理学
An Analysis of World Commission on Environment and Development's *The Brundtland Report, Our Common Future*	解析世界环境与发展委员会《布伦特兰报告：我们共同的未来》	地理学
An Analysis of James E. Lovelock's *Gaia: A New Look at Life on Earth*	解析詹姆斯·E. 拉伍洛克《盖娅：地球生命的新视野》	地理学
An Analysis of Paul Kennedy's *The Rise and Fall of the Great Powers: Economic Change and Military Conflict from 1500—2000*	解析保罗·肯尼迪《大国的兴衰：1500—2000 年的经济变革与军事冲突》	历史
An Analysis of Janet L. Abu-Lughod's *Before European Hegemony: The World System A. D. 1250—1350*	解析珍妮特·L. 阿布-卢格霍德《欧洲霸权之前：1250—1350 年的世界体系》	历史
An Analysis of Alfred W. Crosby's *The Columbian Exchange: Biological and Cultural Consequences of 1492*	解析艾尔弗雷德·W. 克罗斯比《哥伦布大交换：1492 以后的生物影响和文化冲击》	历史
An Analysis of Tony Judt's *Postwar: A History of Europe since 1945*	解析托尼·朱特《战后欧洲史》	历史
An Analysis of Richard J. Evans's *In Defence of History*	解析理查德·J. 艾文斯《捍卫历史》	历史
An Analysis of Eric Hobsbawm's *The Age of Revolution: Europe 1789–1848*	解析艾瑞克·霍布斯鲍姆《革命的年代：欧洲 1789—1848 年》	历史

An Analysis of Roland Barthes's *Mythologies*	解析罗兰·巴特《神话学》	文学与批判理论
An Analysis of Simon de Beauvoir's *The Second Sex*	解析西蒙娜·德·波伏娃《第二性》	文学与批判理论
An Analysis of Edward W. Said's *Orientalism*	解析爱德华·W. 萨义德《东方主义》	文学与批判理论
An Analysis of Virginia Woolf's *A Room of One's Own*	解析弗吉尼亚·伍尔芙《一间自己的房间》	文学与批判理论
An Analysis of Judith Butler's *Gender Trouble*	解析朱迪斯·巴特勒《性别麻烦》	文学与批判理论
An Analysis of Ferdinand de Saussure's *Course in General Linguistics*	解析费尔迪南·德·索绪尔《普通语言学教程》	文学与批判理论
An Analysis of Susan Sontag's *On Photography*	解析苏珊·桑塔格《论摄影》	文学与批判理论
An Analysis of Walter Benjamin's *The Work of Art in the Age of Mechanical Reproduction*	解析瓦尔特·本雅明《机械复制时代的艺术作品》	文学与批判理论
An Analysis of W.E.B. Du Bois's *The Souls of Black Folk*	解析 W.E.B. 杜波依斯《黑人的灵魂》	文学与批判理论
An Analysis of Plato's *The Republic*	解析柏拉图《理想国》	哲学
An Analysis of Plato's *Symposium*	解析柏拉图《会饮篇》	哲学
An Analysis of Aristotle's *Metaphysics*	解析亚里士多德《形而上学》	哲学
An Analysis of Aristotle's *Nicomachean Ethics*	解析亚里士多德《尼各马可伦理学》	哲学
An Analysis of Immanuel Kant's *Critique of Pure Reason*	解析伊曼努尔·康德《纯粹理性批判》	哲学
An Analysis of Ludwig Wittgenstein's *Philosophical Investigations*	解析路德维希·维特根斯坦《哲学研究》	哲学
An Analysis of G.W.F. Hegel's *Phenomenology of Spirit*	解析 G.W.F. 黑格尔《精神现象学》	哲学
An Analysis of Baruch Spinoza's *Ethics*	解析巴鲁赫·斯宾诺莎《伦理学》	哲学
An Analysis of Hannah Arendt's *The Human Condition*	解析汉娜·阿伦特《人的境况》	哲学
An Analysis of G.E.M. Anscombe's *Modern Moral Philosophy*	解析 G.E.M. 安斯康姆《现代道德哲学》	哲学
An Analysis of David Hume's *An Enquiry Concerning Human Understanding*	解析大卫·休谟《人类理解研究》	哲学

An Analysis of Søren Kierkegaard's *Fear and Trembling*	解析索伦·克尔凯郭尔《恐惧与战栗》	哲学
An Analysis of René Descartes's *Meditations on First Philosophy*	解析勒内·笛卡尔《第一哲学沉思录》	哲学
An Analysis of Friedrich Nietzsche's *On the Genealogy of Morality*	解析弗里德里希·尼采《论道德的谱系》	哲学
An Analysis of Gilbert Ryle's *The Concept of Mind*	解析吉尔伯特·赖尔《心的概念》	哲学
An Analysis of Thomas Kuhn's *The Structure of Scientific Revolutions*	解析托马斯·库恩《科学革命的结构》	哲学
An Analysis of John Stuart Mill's *Utilitarianism*	解析约翰·斯图亚特·穆勒《功利主义》	哲学
An Analysis of Aristotle's *Politics*	解析亚里士多德《政治学》	政治学
An Analysis of Niccolò Machiavelli's *The Prince*	解析尼科洛·马基雅维利《君主论》	政治学
An Analysis of Karl Marx's *Capital*	解析卡尔·马克思《资本论》	政治学
An Analysis of Benedict Anderson's *Imagined Communities*	解析本尼迪克特·安德森《想象的共同体》	政治学
An Analysis of Samuel P. Huntington's *The Clash of Civilizations and the Remaking of World Order*	解析塞缪尔·P.亨廷顿《文明的冲突与世界秩序重建》	政治学
An Analysis of Alexis de Tocqueville's *Democracy in America*	解析阿列克西·德·托克维尔《论美国的民主》	政治学
An Analysis of John A. Hobson's *Imperialism: A Study*	解析约翰·A.霍布森《帝国主义》	政治学
An Analysis of Thomas Paine's *Common Sense*	解析托马斯·潘恩《常识》	政治学
An Analysis of John Rawls's *A Theory of Justice*	解析约翰·罗尔斯《正义论》	政治学
An Analysis of Francis Fukuyama's *The End of History and the Last Man*	解析弗朗西斯·福山《历史的终结与最后的人》	政治学
An Analysis of John Locke's *Two Treatises of Government*	解析约翰·洛克《政府论》	政治学
An Analysis of Sun Tzu's *The Art of War*	解析孙武《孙子兵法》	政治学
An Analysis of Henry Kissinger's *World Order: Reflections on the Character of Nations and the Course of History*	解析亨利·基辛格《世界秩序》	政治学
An Analysis of Jean-Jacques Rousseau's *The Social Contract*	解析让-雅克·卢梭《社会契约论》	政治学

英文书名	中文书名	学科
An Analysis of Odd Arne Westad's *The Global Cold War: Third World Interventions and the Making of Our Times*	解析文安立《全球冷战：美苏对第三世界的干涉与当代世界的形成》	政治学
An Analysis of Sigmund Freud's *The Interpretation of Dreams*	解析西格蒙德·弗洛伊德《梦的解析》	心理学
An Analysis of William James' *The Principles of Psychology*	解析威廉·詹姆斯《心理学原理》	心理学
An Analysis of Philip Zimbardo's *The Lucifer Effect*	解析菲利普·津巴多《路西法效应》	心理学
An Analysis of Leon Festinger's *A Theory of Cognitive Dissonance*	解析利昂·费斯汀格《认知失调论》	心理学
An Analysis of Richard H. Thaler & Cass R. Sunstein's *Nudge: Improving Decisions about Health, Wealth, and Happiness*	解析理查德·H. 泰勒/卡斯·R. 桑斯坦《助推：如何做出有关健康、财富和幸福的更优决策》	心理学
An Analysis of Gordon Allport's *The Nature of Prejudice*	解析高尔登·奥尔波特《偏见的本质》	心理学
An Analysis of Steven Pinker's *The Better Angels of Our Nature: Why Violence Has Declined*	解析斯蒂芬·平克《人性中的善良天使：暴力为什么会减少》	心理学
An Analysis of Stanley Milgram's *Obedience to Authority*	解析斯坦利·米尔格拉姆《对权威的服从》	心理学
An Analysis of Betty Friedan's *The Feminine Mystique*	解析贝蒂·弗里丹《女性的奥秘》	心理学
An Analysis of David Riesman's *The Lonely Crowd: A Study of the Changing American Character*	解析大卫·理斯曼《孤独的人群：美国人社会性格演变之研究》	社会学
An Analysis of Franz Boas's *Race, Language and Culture*	解析弗朗兹·博厄斯《种族、语言与文化》	社会学
An Analysis of Pierre Bourdieu's *Outline of a Theory of Practice*	解析皮埃尔·布尔迪厄《实践理论大纲》	社会学
An Analysis of Max Weber's *The Protestant Ethic and the Spirit of Capitalism*	解析马克斯·韦伯《新教伦理与资本主义精神》	社会学
An Analysis of Jane Jacobs's *The Death and Life of Great American Cities*	解析简·雅各布斯《美国大城市的死与生》	社会学
An Analysis of C. Wright Mills's *The Sociological Imagination*	解析C. 赖特·米尔斯《社会学的想象力》	社会学
An Analysis of Robert E. Lucas Jr.'s *Why Doesn't Capital Flow from Rich to Poor Countries?*	解析小罗伯特·E. 卢卡斯《为何资本不从富国流向穷国？》	社会学

An Analysis of Émile Durkheim's *On Suicide*	解析埃米尔·迪尔凯姆《自杀论》	社会学
An Analysis of Eric Hoffer's *The True Believer: Thoughts on the Nature of Mass Movements*	解析埃里克·霍弗《狂热分子：群众运动圣经》	社会学
An Analysis of Jared M. Diamond's *Collapse: How Societies Choose to Fail or Survive*	解析贾雷德·M.戴蒙德《大崩溃：社会如何选择兴亡》	社会学
An Analysis of Michel Foucault's *The History of Sexuality Vol. 1: The Will to Knowledge*	解析米歇尔·福柯《性史（第一卷）：求知意志》	社会学
An Analysis of Michel Foucault's *Discipline and Punish*	解析米歇尔·福柯《规训与惩罚》	社会学
An Analysis of Richard Dawkins's *The Selfish Gene*	解析理查德·道金斯《自私的基因》	社会学
An Analysis of Antonio Gramsci's *Prison Notebooks*	解析安东尼奥·葛兰西《狱中札记》	社会学
An Analysis of Augustine's *Confessions*	解析奥古斯丁《忏悔录》	神学
An Analysis of C.S. Lewis's *The Abolition of Man*	解析C.S.路易斯《人之废》	神学

图书在版编目（CIP）数据

解析路德维希·维特根斯坦《哲学研究》: 汉、英 / 迈克尔·奥沙利文
（Michael O'Sullivan）著; 杨晓波译.
— 上海: 上海外语教育出版社, 2019
（世界思想宝库钥匙丛书）
ISBN 978-7-5446-5960-4

Ⅰ. ①解… Ⅱ. ①迈… ②杨… Ⅲ. ①维特根斯坦（Wittgenstein, Ludwig 1889—1951）—哲学思想—思想评论—汉、英 Ⅳ. ①B561.59

中国版本图书馆CIP数据核字（2019）第000000号

This Chinese-English bilingual edition of *An Analysis of Ludwig Wittgenstein's Philosophical Investigations* is published by arrangement with Macat International Limited.
Licensed for sale throughout the world.

本书汉英双语版由Macat国际有限公司授权上海外语教育出版社有限公司出版。
供在全世界范围内发行、销售。

图字：09 – 2018 – 549

出版发行：**上海外语教育出版社**
（上海外国语大学内） 邮编：200083
电　　话：021-65425300（总机）
电子邮箱：bookinfo@sflep.com.cn
网　　址：http://www.sflep.com
责任编辑：孙　玉

印　刷:	上海信老印刷厂
开　本:	890×1240　1/32　印张 5.625　字数 116千字
版　次:	2019年11月第1版　2019年11月第1次印刷
印　数:	2 100 册
书　号:	ISBN 978-7-5446-5960-4
定　价:	30.00 元

本版图书如有印装质量问题，可向本社调换
质量服务热线：4008-213-263　电子邮箱：editorial@sflep.com